Haunted
Virginia

Haunted
Virginia

Ghosts and Strange Phenomena of the Old Dominion

L. B. Taylor Jr.

Illustrations by Heather Adel Wiggins

STACKPOLE
BOOKS

Published by
STACKPOLE BOOKS
5067 Ritter Road
Mechanicsburg, PA 17055
www.stackpolebooks.com

Printed in the United States of America

10 9 8 7 6 5 4 3 2 1

FIRST EDITION

Design by Beth Oberholtzer
Cover design by Caroline Stover

Library of Congress Cataloging-in-Publication Data

Taylor, L. B.
    Haunted Virginia : ghosts and strange phenomena of the Old Dominion / L.B. Taylor, Jr. — 1st ed.
      p.   cm.
    Includes bibliographical references (p.).
    ISBN-13: 978-0-8117-3541-4 (pbk.)
    ISBN-10: 0-8117-3541-9 (pbk.)
    1. Ghosts—Virginia. 2. Haunted places—Virginia. I. Title.
BF1472.U6T3955   2009
133.109755—dc22
                                                      2008035174

Contents

Introduction

VIRGINIA ABOUNDS IN GHOSTS. IN FACT, IT MAY WELL BE THE MOST haunted state in America, and for good reason—it is the oldest colony in the New World, with a history dating back more than four hundred years. It is likely that more tragedy and trauma have occurred here than anywhere else in the country. The seventeenth and eighteenth centuries saw fierce Indian attacks, as well as the Revolutionary War. During the Civil War, more battles were fought and more men died prematurely in Virginia than in any other state.

The commonwealth still has a great number of old houses, manor homes, mansions, and plantations dating back to the 1700s and 1800s, which seem to frequently provide fertile ground for the return of spirits. In addition, Virginians have had a keen sense of history and tradition, and from the early settlers on, they have carefully preserved and passed down lore and legends from generation to generation, including numerous accounts of ghostly activity.

Are ghosts real? Who can say? Humankind has debated their existence for more than four thousand years. Certainly a great percentage of alleged hauntings can be explained away by scientific and rational means. Common sense and the application of simple logic can clear up most mysteries. But not all. Some extraordinary happenings simply defy explanation. And skeptical arguments are limited by the boundaries of human understanding. Can anyone say for certain that there is not a psychic realm that still lurks in the dark recesses of the unknown, the key to which may be found sometime in the future?

Well-respected author and ghost expert Hans Holzer may have said it best when he noted: "Throughout the centuries, the skeptical, the scientific and the credulous have attempted to solve the enigma of ghosts. There are theories, but no proofs, as to why things happen. But that the incidence of such happenings exceeds the laws of probability, and that their number establishes that there is something to investigate, is beyond dispute."

Perhaps Dunninger, the great television magician of a couple generations ago, summed it up as well as anyone: "To those who believe, no explanation is necessary. To those who don't believe, no explanation is possible." And from the pen of the renowned author H. P. Lovecraft, "There is something marvelous beyond the horizon of death and the limit of our sight."

Whether or not you believe in the supernatural, the incidents described in this volume offer a sampling of the colorful legends and traditions of Virginia. Here then is a choice blend of the macabre, the scary, the inexplicable, and in some instances of perceived phantoms, the humorous.

Enjoy!

Northern
Virginia

FROM THE OUTSKIRTS OF WASHINGTON, D.C., RUNNING SOUTH AND west is the heavily populated region of Northern Virginia. Included in these hallowed grounds are such historic places as Mount Vernon, George Washington's home, and the great Civil War battlefields at Manassas and Fredericksburg, where thousands of heroic young men died well before their time. Here too are Arlington National Cemetery and other sacred burial sites. In Old Town Alexandria, Fairfax, Leesburg, and other areas are thousands of ancient houses with histories going back hundreds of years. All of these types of locales are thought to be some of the most fertile grounds for the presence of spectral entities still trapped within earth's bounds.

The Snipping Poltergeist

One of the most bizarre episodes in the history of psychic phenomena in America occurred more than two hundred years ago at the tiny crossroads town of Middleway, West Virginia, north of Winchester. It is included in this volume because at the time, Middleway was still part of Virginia. The happenings that occurred here have been covered extensively in the media and were attested to at the time by scores of eyewitnesses, some of whom traveled long distances to see for themselves. Alfred E. Smith, a respected twentieth-century magazine editor, called it "the truest ghost story ever told."

In 1790, Adam Livingston moved with his family from Lancaster, Pennsylvania, to the then-remote area of Jefferson County, Virginia. He bought a seventy-acre farm and began carving out a living in the wilderness. On a stormy, windswept night four years later, a stranger knocked at Livingston's door and asked for refuge for the evening from the heavy rain.

During the night, the man suddenly became seriously ill, and it appeared that he was dying. He asked his startled host if he could have a Catholic priest come to the house to administer his last rites. Livingston's wife, a devout Lutheran, told her husband she would not have a Catholic priest in her house, and anyway, the farmer didn't know where to find one in the first place.

Soon after, the stranger died. Livingston arranged for the body to be placed in a crude coffin in his house to await burial. As was the custom in that day, he asked a neighbor to come over to "sit up with the dead." That evening, a succession of strange happenings began. The two men lit several candles as darkness fell, but then stepped back in fright as they were snuffed out by what seemed to be unseen hands. There was no wind or any other natural cause for the extinguishment. The men relit the candles several times, and the same thing happened. The neighbor was so shaken that he immediately left.

Following the burial the next afternoon, Livingston and his family returned home and built a roaring fire in their fireplace. Inexplicably, the fire flared up, and blazing logs leaped from the fireplace and whirled around the floor in a weird dance. Showers of sparks and glowing embers cascaded over the handmade rug, and Livingston and his wife jumped about, stomping them out. Each time they returned a log, it mysteriously hopped out again. This continued through most of the night and then suddenly stopped. The farmer and his wife collapsed on their beds, physically, mentally, and emotionally exhausted.

The next night, the perplexed farmer awoke to the thundering sounds of a herd of horses galloping around the house. He roused his wife and they looked outside. The moon was bright, but they saw nothing. Yet the sounds continued off and on for more than an hour, and the couple spent another restless night.

As the days and weeks passed, the terrifying manifestations intensified. Inside the house, showers of hot stones, appearing out of nowhere, sailed through the air; dishes and cooking utensils were tossed about by invisible hands; and heavy pieces of furniture moved across rooms, untouched by any mortal. At night, footsteps were heard, and flashes of what seemed to be ghostly apparitions materialized. Livingston's savings, a fairly large sum of money, disappeared from a locked chest in his bedroom.

Nor were the supernatural activities confined indoors. One day, while walking down a dirt road that passed by his house, the beleaguered farmer was confronted by an irate man on a wagon. The man demanded to know why Livingston had stretched a rope across the road, impeding passage. Livingston thought the man was either drunk or crazy. He saw no rope. Then the man leaped down from his wagon, took out a large hunting knife, and began slashing madly at the unseen rope. Another man in a buggy came up, and he too cursed the farmer, demanding to know why there was a rope across the road. He also tried to cut it with a knife and became frustrated at slicing through the thin air. Livingston finally suggested they get back in their wagon and buggy and drive their horses through the phantom rope, which, to their amazement, they did.

Word soon spread through the region that some very curious things were happening at the Livingston farm. Many began to believe that it was infested with demons, a conjecture fueled by the fact that the farmer's animals, including cattle, horses, hogs, and other stock, began dying of unexplained causes.

All of this, however, odd as it was, served merely as a prelude to what happened next. Out of nowhere, an eerie clipping sound began to be heard. It was like the sound made by an invisible pair of giant tailor's shears. And they were destructive shears. Wielded by indiscernible hands, they cut crescent-shaped holes in the family's clothes, in blankets and sheets, even in leather boots. This created an even greater stir in the community, and people came from miles around to catch a glimpse of the Devil at work. Many were not disappointed.

One woman who came to the farmhouse, upon leaving, discovered that the ghostly scissors had cut half-moon-shaped holes in her valuable Oriental shawl. Another lady, who had come from Winchester, took the precaution of carefully wrapping her handsome new cap inside a silk handkerchief before entering the house. Later, she found it had been cut to ribbons. A skeptical man arrived one day in his new swallowtail coat and denounced the proceedings as a hoax. As he departed, he looked down and was shocked to see that the tails of his coat had been neatly snipped off!

One day three young men arrived and proclaimed they had come a long way to face the Devil himself if he was the author of these things. They left the farmhouse abruptly when the hearth-stone in the room in which they were sitting arose from its place and whirled around the room. On another occasion, a woman visiting Mrs. Livingston was strolling in the yard with her, admiring her fine flock of ducks. Suddenly they heard the dreaded "snip, snip" sound and looked on in total astonishment as, one by one, each duck's head was clipped off by the diabolical shears. It is recorded that other witnesses saw this incredible sight.

And still the curious came. One was a local German tailor who announced that all the proclaimed occurrences were the result of stupid superstition and wild imagination. Then he happened to pass by the bewitched farm one day carrying a package containing a suit he had made for a neighbor. He heard a loud "clip, clip" sound about his head and, nonplussed, shouted at the unseen noise to "go to damn." When he arrived at the house of the man he had made the suit for, he unwrapped the package and found the cloth full of crescent-shaped slits and utterly ruined.

The weirdness had been going on for about three months when, one night, Livingston had a vivid dream. He envisioned himself climbing up a steep mountain. When he reached the top, he saw a man dressed in clerical robes, and he heard a voice saying, "This is the man who can help you." He believed the dream to be an omen. He then began a fevered search to find the man in the robes. Eventually he was led to a man named Richard McSherry, a Catholic. With McSherry's help, he met the Reverend Dennis Cahill, a Roman Catholic missionary priest. Livingston immediately recognized him as the man in his dream.

With the corroborative testimony of others who knew of the demonic activities going on at his farm, Livingston was finally able to persuade the priest to help him. At first the efforts of sprinkling holy water in the house seemed to have no effect; the clipping sounds continued unabated.

The next day, however, Father Cahill performed a mass in the very room where the stranger had died three months earlier. With this, the clipping ceased. As the priest was about to leave the house, one last otherworldly manifestation materialized. As the father had set one foot over the doorsill and the other in the hall, the money that had disappeared from Livingston's chest earlier suddenly appeared between his feet.

And with that, the ninety-day onslaught of poltergeist activity halted as abruptly as it had began. Livingston was so overcome at the deliverance from whatever evil spirit had plagued him and his family that he and his wife converted to Catholicism, and he subsequently deeded thirty-four acres of his farmland, still known as Priest's Field, to the Catholic Church with the understanding that a chapel would be built there.

Today no trace of the old farmhouse remains. Yet the legend still lives. And the town, although officially called Middleway, is better known, and more often referred to, as Wizard's Clip.

The Enduring Legend of the Female Stranger

One of the highlight stops on the popular ghost tour of Old Town Alexandria is the richly historic Gadsby's Tavern at Royal and Cameron Streets. It has been a well-liked watering hole for nearly 250 years. In its heyday in the late 1700s, it hosted many of the most famous figures of the early Republic, including the man who seemed to get around to just about every place in Virginia—George Washington.

The original house dates from 1770, and the large, three-story section, the ultimate in elegance and comfort for its time, was opened by a man named John Wise in 1792. The building was named for John Gadsby, who operated a tavern from 1796 to 1808. It was at this site that Washington, in 1775, presided at a meeting that led to the adoption of the first document asserting Colonial rights, the Fairfax Resolves. During the American Revolution, many important meetings and discussions were held here by such gentleman patriots as John Paul Jones, George Clinton, and Benjamin Franklin, not to mention Baron de Kalb and Lafayette.

Under the genial guidance of Gadsby, who had been an English pubkeeper, the fame of his establishment's hospitality spread, it is said, from New York to New Orleans. With such an auspicious background, it is little wonder that the tavern's ballroom wood-work is now displayed at the Metropolitan Museum of Art in New York City. The rest of the complex has survived pretty much intact and has been handsomely restored.

Gadsby's also is the scene of the spectral return of a beautiful young woman, a woman of consummate mystery, who died there in 1816 under the most suspect of circumstances. Ever since, visitors have reported seeing her looking out a bedroom window, holding a candle. Others have spotted her walking the halls or standing by her tombstone nearby. Intrigue and legend over who she was and why she reappears in ghostly form have swirled around the tavern for nearly two hundred years.

The most common theory is that when she and her husband sailed into the Alexandria port in October 1816, she already was deathly ill. She was taken to Gadsby's and treated by a doctor and several nurses. When it became evident that she was not going to recover, her husband asked everyone involved to promise never to reveal the lady's identity. She died a few days later and was buried in St. Paul's Cemetery. A finely carved tabletop tombstone read, "In memory of the female stranger, died Oct. 14, 1816, age 23 years 8 months." Soon after, the "husband" inexplicably disappeared without out paying his bills, including $1,500 for the tombstone.

Speculative versions about the woman's identity abounded in the city for years, and still go on. Some believed her to be the daughter of Aaron Burr, the man who shot Alexander Hamilton in a duel. Others ascribed to the contention that she was one of four orphaned children who were separated from each other at a young age. Many years later, she unknowingly married her own brother, and she didn't want the horrible secret to be revealed.

Another popular offering, told by ghost tour guides, is that she was the ward of an English nobleman who had fallen in love with her. He was seventy-five, and she but twenty-three. She loved him too, but like a father. The nobleman allegedly walked into the garden at an undisclosed location one day and found her in the arms of a British officer. The old man reacted violently, and when he attacked the lover, he was pushed hard, fell, hit his head, and died.

The frightened couple then got on a ship and sailed to Alexandria, although she took sick en route and never recovered.

The mysterious woman's most notable appearance came one evening a few years ago, when a man said he saw her in the tavern ballroom. He followed her upstairs to what had been her bedroom, where she disappeared. It was dark, but in the corner of the room was a lit candle in a hurricane lamp. He picked it up and searched the premises but found nothing. Then it dawned on him—what was a lit candle doing in the deserted room? He raced downstairs and got the tavern manager to go back up with him. When they got there, not only was the candle not lit, but the wick was still white, as if it never had been lit. The manager thought the man either was seeing things or had imbibed too much that night.

As he left the room, the man who had witnessed the apparition felt the lamp. It burned his fingers!

A Spectral Summons for Help

The following narrative is extracted from an old family history written more than half a century ago. Out of privacy concerns, the details, such as names and exact locations, are not revealed, although the incident described is believed to have occurred in the mid-nineteenth century in Northern Virginia. It was passed along from generation to generation as being a true account.

It was a cold, blustery night in the dead of winter. The priest was bone-tired from a long day's work. He took off his shoes and stretched out in a comfortable chair before a crackling fire in the rectory. He was alone, and in the silence of the house, silent save for the rain pelting down against the windows, he dozed off.

It was well past 11 P.M. when the priest was roused by a persistent noise. At first he presumed it was a branch being blown against the door by the winds of the storm outside. But then he realized it was someone knocking at his front door. Who could it be at this hour? he wondered. He didn't want to get up, but he knew he had to. If someone was in trouble—and what else could it be on such a bleak night?—it was his job to listen and to help if he could.

He opened the door, and there, under a large umbrella, were two small children, a boy and a girl. Surprised, the priest asked where they had come from, but they answered only that they had come for him. They said their father was very ill and needed him. The priest asked if it couldn't wait until morning, but when he read the anguished looks on their faces, he answered his own question.

He asked them to come inside while he put on his shoes and got his coat and hat, but they steadfastly refused to enter, saying they would wait outside. This disturbed the priest, because the weather was so nasty, but there was something about these children—something that told him not to insist.

In a few minutes, he returned to the door and told the boy and girl to lead the way and he would follow. They moved very rapidly, and he had a difficult time keeping up with them. They walked briskly several blocks away from the rectory and toward a poor section of town. Finally they arrived at the entrance to a tenement, and then waited to make sure the priest would follow. Inside the building, they climbed a steep flight of stairs and went down a darkened hallway, and then the priest saw the children go into a room past an opened door through which a dim light shone.

Breathing heavily from the long walk and climb, the priest entered the room. It was completely bare of furniture except for a mattress on the floor in one corner. A small gas flame flickered in an old bracket on the wall. The priest looked around for the girl and boy, but they were nowhere to be seen. It was as if they had suddenly evaporated. Strange.

An old man was lying on the mattress, wrapped in dirty blankets. Even in the poorly lit gloom of the room, the priest instantly realized that the man was dying. He knelt down beside the man and said to him, "You have sent for me and I have come." The old man looked completely puzzled. He whispered, "I didn't send for you. I haven't anyone to send."

"You forget, my son," the priest replied. "You sent your little boy and girl through all the rain to bring me here." There was a long moment of silence, and then the man answered.

"Oh, no, father! How could I send them? They died thirty years ago!"

The Librarian Who Will Not Leave

Purcellville, population about twenty-two hundred, is located at the northern tip of Virginia, east of Winchester and twelve miles west of Leesburg. It was here, more than seventy years ago, that a domineering, charismatic woman named Gertrude Robey ruled the local library with an iron fist. She was austere to the extreme, in both appearance and actions. She always dressed in black, sometimes crowned with a broad-brimmed black hat. She could be spotted walking down the street from several blocks away.

Sometime in the 1930s, she persuaded area residents to build a town library that would double as a cultural center. As chief librarian, Gertrude Robey took it upon herself to determine what was readable and what was not for her patrons. Anything in the romance vein with even a hint of eroticism was absolutely banned from her shelves. But she went further than that. Many classics were also deemed unworthy of presentation, and some of these were not sex-oriented, but of historical significance.

Apparently, Gertrude was a Southern sympathizer who recognized that feelings about the Civil War were still touchy. Consequently, one of the volumes she hid was Harriett Beecher Stowe's masterpiece, *Uncle Tom's Cabin*. We know it was hidden because when workmen were building an addition to the library in 1991, twenty-five years after Gertrude died, they found a number of books walled up in an old chimney, Stowe's tome among them.

Although it is now nearly four decades since her passing, Gertrude's presence is still very much felt at the library, both figuratively and literally. "Oh, she's still here," declares present librarian Susie Shackleford. "We get reminders all the time."

One of the most dramatic manifestations comes in the form of a continued rejection of anything even faintly considered off-color. Such well-known authors as Anais Nin and the popular Judith Krantz apparently are considered by Gertrude's spirit to be in this category. Thus, at frequent intervals, such books are chucked off the shelves by unseen hands.

"They don't just fall onto the floor," says Shackleford. "They leap out into the middle of the aisles. There is power behind them." A number of people, browsers and employees alike, have witnessed this ghostly expression of distaste. And it only happens to certain books and specific authors. "It's Gertrude, still letting us know she's around and watching out for what we display," says Shackleford. "Sometimes she also puts books back on the shelves. We've had workers say they hear the sound of books being replaced in the stacks, but when they look to see who is doing it, no one is there. Such reshelving, however, does not include romance novels."

More recently, the spirit critic has given personnel fits over door locks. "I think she does it just to aggravate us," Shackleford notes. "We have a lot of trouble with the locks. One of us will go and unlock a conference room door for, say, a library board meeting, and when the board members go to the room, the door will suddenly be locked. I can't explain it."

This particular trouble began a few years ago, when Gertrude's portrait was removed from its customary place in the library. It had been above a mantel, but when a series of rainstorms caused leaks, a staff member moved the painting—or tried to—to safer quarters. She took it upstairs to a reference room, but the door was unaccountably locked. She then tried the fire doors, which are never locked, but they too were sealed. She went to get the key, but even that wouldn't work. The staffer then became unnerved when, she said, the eyes of Gertrude in the portrait were staring holes through her. Finally they had to call a locksmith.

Others have reported seeing a shadow in the lounge area during hours when the library is closed and no one is in the building. "My favorite is about the electric clock," says Shackleford. "This happened about twelve years ago. The power went out. Gertrude had an old electric clock. Well, it just kept running. Even after I unplugged it and took it down from the wall, it kept on running. An electric clock!"

Gertrude also made her presence felt in 1991 during the building renovations. Apparently she didn't like what the workmen were doing, or how they were doing it. In fact, her disagreements with construction contractors go back more than seventy years. During the original work on the building, she constantly badgered the crews. One day she fell from some scaffolding and broke her leg. She sued the foreman for not forcing her to stay off the scaffolding!

When an addition was being added in 1991, it seems that Gertrude continued her tight vigilance. The contractor said he couldn't get any of his men to work after dark. "They said they kept hearing footsteps above them on the second floor," says Shackle-ford. "Of course, there was no one up there."

Then, when the workers found the cache of forbidden books, they said when they picked them up, their fingers were burned.

"I never knew her in life," says Shackleford. "An older lady here who used to mend books for her said she had a very strong person-ality. She was right. Gertrude ruled this library for over forty years and was sole judge and jury as to what books she felt the public should read. She pretty much likes to remind us from time to time that she still is in charge."

The End of a "Hard" Man

It is believed that two of Virginia's most famous Georges—Wash-ington and Mason—may have had a hand in the design of historic Pohick Church, near Fort Belvoir. They both served on the vestry at the time of its construction, between 1769 and 1774. Much of the building's interior was desecrated by Union troops during the Civil War, when it was used as a stable.

Among the notables buried in the Pohick Cemetery is Richard Chicester, who lived in the eighteenth century. The Chicesters were among the more prominent Colonial families. Although Richard was a respected member of the community, he had a sinister repu-tation among his slaves and was said to have been a cruel master. The slaves were so fearful of him, in fact, that among themselves they called him "Hard" Chicester.

The house servants said that when he died, out from under his bed ran a red rabbit, which was considered at the time an omen of evil. It has been documented that sometime after his burial in the graveyard at Pohick Church, a bolt of lightning struck his tomb-stone and ripped off the first three letters of his first name, "Ric," leaving for all to see, "Hard Chicester."

Another candidate for Virginia's meanest man was an old codger who lived near the village of Singers Glen in Rockingham County early in the twentieth century. He was so mean that his favorite pastime was to sit on his front porch and shoot every bird that alighted on the fence that separated his yard from the road—cardi-nals, blue jays, mockingbirds, it didn't matter. For years, he killed every feathered being that was unfortunate enough to select that particular fence to rest upon.

Eventually the old man came to his own end. On the day of the funeral, his coffin was carried down the road toward the cemetery. As the procession approached the dead man's house, everyone glanced toward the fence. Witnesses said it looked like a live scene out of Alfred Hitchcock's classic horror movie *The Birds*: the fence was lined with every species of bird imaginable, so thick that there was no space between any of them.

Caring Katina of Fall Hill

In 1992, I interviewed a charming woman, then in her mid-nineties, at her historic home, Fall Hill, just outside of Fredericksburg on the scenic Rappahannock River. At the time, Mrs. Lynn W. Franklin was an active area historian with an impeccable memory. A direct descendant of Colonial Governor Alexander Spotswood's wife, she had lived at Fall Hill since 1908. And although the house has a long-standing reputation as being haunted, she never knew fear. "I doubt that you would ever find a more friendly spirit than the one we have here," she said. "In a way, it's actually a comfort to have her here. This house is surrounded by a hundred acres of woods, and it's good to have a ghost with me so no mortals bother us."

The house dates to the latter part of the eighteenth century. *The Virginia Landmarks Register* says it was constructed around 1790, but Mrs. Franklin thinks it may have been built as early as 1763. The legend of the benevolent spirit at Fall Hill has its origins in Williamsburg, where a young Indian girl, whom some said was a Sioux princess, was captured and given to Governor Spotswood. Her name was Katina. When the governor retired in 1720, he moved his residence to Germanna, west of Fredericksburg, and took the Indian maiden with him. She became the nanny for his four children.

After Spotswood died in 1740, Katina went to work for the Thornton family at the site where Fall Hill now stands. "But she was much more than a servant," Mrs. Franklin said. "She was the essence of dedication and devotion to the young ones she loved, and they loved her. The small, dark, and lithesome Katina taught the young Thorntons the ways of the Indian and how best to appreciate nature's beautiful secrets."

Katina died in 1777 and was buried in the garden. "When I first came to Fall Hill to live, I was nine years old," said Mrs. Franklin. "My grandfather took me by the hand one day and said, 'I'm going to show you the grave of our old family nurse.' We knelt beside a little grave covered by a granite stone. Nothing was written on it. My grandfather then told me that when his great-grandfather lived, Katina brought him up and taught him to speak Indian. She was a very old woman then, and when she died, he was inconsolable. He wept and said he had lost his best friend."

Exactly when the apparition of Katina first appeared, allegedly to make sure that young descendants of the Thornton family were being properly cared for, is not certain, though recorded reports of her sightings go back to the early years of the twentieth century. When Mrs. Bessie Taylor Robinson lived in the house in the 1920s, she said that many persons had spoken of seeing Katina walking about the plantation as though looking for her companions of long ago.

One of the first occurrences Mrs. Robinson remembered was when her two boys were home from school and were sleeping in the nursery. The next morning, one of the youngsters came downstairs, appearing quite pale. He asked his mother if she had come into their room the previous night to cover them. She said she hadn't and inquired why he asked. He told her that an old woman with long, black braids had come in during the night, and then disappeared through the wall at the head of the bed.

In 1938, a young woman came to visit Fall Hill. According to Mrs. Franklin, "One afternoon she was taking a nap upstairs. She awoke around 5 P.M. and started to get up, when she saw a young boy dressed in knee britches walk through the closed door. Following behind him was a little Indian woman, with long, black, braided hair. The woman thought some children in the house had dressed up to amuse her. But when she addressed them, there was no answer. They just disappeared. There were no children in the house at the time. She'd seen the ghost of Katina!"

On another occasion, Mrs. Robinson saw the apparition. She arrived home late one night, and as she stood in the downstairs hall, she witnessed a figure coming out of the room where her younger son was sleeping. Upon examination, Mrs. Robinson found every other member of the family sound asleep, and all the doors and windows were locked shut.

Several years ago, Mrs. Franklin had her own ethereal experience, in her bedroom. "I was in bed," she recalled, "wide awake, reading. I had my little granddaughter in the house with me. We'd just recently lost her father, and it was a period of considerable stress. I had never seen a ghost of any description before, although, of course, I was well aware of the stories about Katina. I never thought I would see her, and to be truthful, I was never quite convinced that anyone had ever seen her. Imagination can do a lot of things, you know.

"But I definitely wasn't dreaming. I was alert. Then, suddenly, at the foot of my bed there appeared this darkly beautiful face. She just looked at me with those dark Indian eyes. Her expression never changed, but it seemed like she had a look of great concern. I interpreted it to mean that I had better take good care of my granddaughter. She was there just for an instant, and then she was gone. But I have no question that she was real."

Mrs. Franklin said that those who claimed to have seen the Indian ghost most often saw her near the top of the stairs, where she vanishes from sight by apparently walking through a bedroom wall.

"Years ago, we stripped off the old wallpaper in that room," Mrs. Franklin noted. "We discovered that during the 1800s, there were some alterations made in the house. At the spot where Katina appears to walk through the wall, there was, under the wallpaper, an old, sealed-up doorway. It was a second door to that bedroom.

"I believe it was once the nursery!"

The Cat with Ten Lives

Ed Barr of Woodbridge tells a wonderful tale about his beloved pet cat, Katherine. "It is written someplace that animals have a soul as well as a spirit," he says. "This is the story of one of them. Katherine came to our home in a roundabout way. Our granddaughter rescued her from the streets. My grandson, being young at the time and playing with toy cars and soldiers, would at times find some of them missing. He observed the cat walking down the hall with a soldier in her mouth one day, only to appear a few minutes later without it. Several years later, when moving to another house, the family found a hole in the bottom covering of my grandson's box spring, and there, in the corner, lay all his lost toys."

After Ed's grandchildren grew up and left home, his daughter moved in with him and his wife, and she brought Katherine with her. "She was playful and loving, and ruled the house," Ed says. "My wife, being a quiltmaker, has a closet full of fabric, which we all found out that Katherine loved. When my wife would be at her worktable, the cat would be there too. She had a bad habit of pulling pins out of things with her front teeth, and it was a fight to stop her from swallowing them.

"When my wife would have a quilt in a hoop, Katherine would be on the table waiting for the quilt to be laid flat, and then she would walk on it and lie down. When my wife would finish quilting for the night, she would cover the quilt with an old tablecloth. In the morning, there would be an indentation where the cat had slept on it.

"In our rec room, there is a recliner where I sit to watch television. The cat also liked it. When I would be sitting in it, she would sit on the floor in front of me and stare. If I left the chair for any reason, she would jump onto it, curl up, shut her eyes, and pretend she was asleep. When my wife and I would retire for the night, we would read for a short time and then turn off the lights. Katherine would jump onto the bottom of the bed, walk between us, then go to the bottom of the bed and curl up until we were asleep. Then she would depart in search of an uncovered quilt.

"Eventually Katherine developed some health problems, and we had to put her down. She was close to eighteen years old. One morning shortly after this, our daughter said she had seen the cat in the upstairs hall the night before. We simply said, 'Yes, she still lives here. We see her quite often.' We feel her jump on the bed some nights, and on occasion we can feel her weight at our feet. Although my wife no longer has to cover her work to keep the cat hair off, we see the indentation of Katherine in the middle of the quilt. At times I see her peeking around the leg of the train table or sitting in front of the door.

"The three of us feel she enjoyed her stay with us and likes to come back for a visit. After these visits, we invariably find one or more of her cat hairs at or near the spot where we saw her."

Ed also had another brush with the supernatural. A professional photographer, he once took a photo in Woodlawn Plantation, near Mount Vernon, that neither he nor anyone else has ever satisfactorily explained. He was shooting period furniture in a room in which he was the only living mortal. Yet when his photos were printed, they clearly showed the silhouettes of two booted feet standing beneath a table. He has no idea of whom they belonged to or how they got there.

Purring from Beyond

About seventy years ago, in a small town in Northern Virginia, there lived an eccentric woman affectionately known as "Miss Effie." An elderly spinster, she resided in a small frame house accompanied only by an old, gray cat, unimaginatively named Tom.

She took the feline everywhere, even to church services on Sunday mornings. This caused some consternation, especially to the local preacher, because when Miss Effie stroked Tom on her lap, the cat would purr loudly enough to disrupt the concentration of members during silent prayer ceremonies. Efforts to persuade the old woman to leave Tom at home proved futile. She countered that certain males in the congregation snored louder than her cherished pet purred.

Finally, at the ripe old age of eighteen, Tom passed on. This spurred a round of spirited speculation among the townspeople. They all wondered whether the grief-stricken Miss Effie would attend church services the following Sunday. Consequently, the building was packed. Everyone sneaked glances toward where Miss Effie was seated. Then there were gasps. It appeared that she was stroking something invisible on her lap. The woman, they thought, had gone mad. Could she possibly think Tom had been resurrected? There was a stir of murmurs among the pews.

After a rousing sermon, the preacher called for a moment of silent prayer. It was then that everyone craned their necks, opened their eyes, and stared, with open mouths, toward Miss Effie. As she continued to stroke, the distinct and unmistakable sound of a cat purring was heard throughout the building.

It was so loud, some declared, that the church windows rattled.

Edgar Allan Poe, the Virginian

Edgar Allan Poe, the great author and poet, was not born in Virginia, but he is considered by native Virginians to be one of their own. Although he lived at times in Maryland and New York, he was raised in the Old Dominion, attended the University of Virginia, and spent most of his short life in the commonwealth. There are, too, vague reports that his spirit may occasionally visit an old house on West Grace Street in Richmond where he gave his last public reading of his classic work "The Raven."

The following account, involving a fascinating series of incidents that occurred early in the nineteenth century, collaterally involving Poe, is excerpted and recounted with the permission of *Fate* magazine.

Lieutenant Robert F. Massie of Northern Virginia was stationed at Fort Independence, Massachusetts, in 1817. He was a popular young officer. One evening, however, following an argument over a card game, Massie was challenged to a duel. He was ill-equipped for such a fight with a master swordsman, and he was killed in an attempt to defend his honor. He was buried on Castle Island.

The man who ran him in was in turn despised by his fellow officers, and they plotted to seek revenge. He mysteriously disappeared shortly afterward. Ten years later, in May 1827, a young man who went by the name of Edgar A. Perry enlisted in the Army and was sent to Castle Island. Upon viewing Massie's grave, Perry inquired about his death and what happened to his killer.

He was told about the duel and what had occurred afterward. One night, a group of officers got the survivor drunk. They then took him down to the lowest dungeon in the fort, forced him into a small casement, shackled him to the floor—and walled up the narrow opening to the windowless cell.

In 1905, while restoring the old fortress, workmen broke open a wall and found a skeleton covered with fragments of an old Army uniform dating to the 1820s.

Meanwhile, Massie's body was moved in 1892 to Governors Island. It was dug up again in 1908 and taken to Deer Island when Boston's Logan International Airport was being built. His remains were disinterred once more in 1939 and taken to Fort Devens in

Ayer, Massachusetts. Finally, some years later, a delegation of "concerned Southern citizens" had his body exhumed yet another time and sent back to Virginia, where he now at last rests. He had been disturbed so much that his remains became known as the "Bouncing Body of Boston Bay." One would think Massie had good reason to return for a ghostly protest, but there are no accounts of his reappearance.

The man who killed him, and then met his own gruesome death by being walled up alive in the dank dungeon, turned out to be the real-life inspiration for one of the greatest horror stories in short American fiction. It was he whom the young man called Edgar A. Perry wrote about when he penned "The Cask of Amontillado."

Edgar A. Perry was the Army enlistment name used by Edgar Allan Poe.

The Shenandoah Valley

THE GREAT SHENANDOAH VALLEY RUNS SOUTH FROM ITS NORTHERN TIP at Winchester down to Lexington, where Civil War generals Robert E. Lee and Stonewall Jackson, who fought in so many historic battles along this scenic corridor, are buried. Here, in the shadows of the majestic Blue Ridge Mountains, are the rich agricultural regions, the "breadbasket of the Confederacy." And here too are the folklore traditions brought south by the Pennsylvania Dutch, ranging from herbal medicines and natural cures to stark fear of ghosts and the Devil himself—lore that has been well preserved through the centuries.

Nearer My God to Thee

Early in the twentieth century, two spinster sisters, Annie and Ellie Benson, lived with their niece, Marie Mullins, in a rambling old manor house in the shadows of the mountains in the northern part of the Shenandoah Valley, between Warrenton and Front Royal. The sisters were said to be psychically sensitive. Paranormal activity seemed to swirl around them.

Some of the extraordinary incidents in their lives were recorded several years ago in *Beyond the Limit of Our Sight*, by Elizabeth Biggs, who has graciously granted permission to recount one such event, which occurred in 1920. A quarrelsome couple named Ward and Willa Price lived in a house in the Bensons' neighborhood. There was much community gossip about the Prices, who fought openly and often. At times their verbal feuds carried out into the street, and details were soon relayed from house to house. Willa was known as a shrew of a woman who reviled and bedeviled her long-suffering husband at the slightest opportunity, no matter who was listening.

One day, Ward, who apparently had taken enough abuse, stood at the top of the stairs in their house and shouted profanities at his wife. He was so upset that he lost his balance, fell headlong down the stairs, broke his neck, and died on the spot. As was the custom in those days, the coffin containing the body was placed in the house, and friends and neighbors came to bring food and try to comfort Willa.

During casual conversations, people recalled how much Ward had loved his church. He had a beautiful singing voice and took great pride in singing solos with the choir. Some thought it was his religious fervor that had caused the couple's relationship to crumble, as Willa had come to resent Ward's dedication to the church and especially his love of singing hymns.

The day of the funeral, Annie, Ellie, and Marie all went to the Price house to help out. The dining room was filled with flowers, and mourners packed the place. The Benson sisters saw an odd-looking item in a corner of the room. It was an antique gramophone machine with a crank handle, so full of dust that it obviously hadn't been used for years. They found records in a nearby cabinet, neatly stored in pigeonhole sections, but none in the machine. They recalled that Ward had loved to play his favorite hymns on the records—that was, until a few years earlier, when Willa had screamed at him to turn the infernal machine off.

It was, everyone remembered, a bizarre day. Willa would not be consoled and announced that she was going to remain in her room upstairs, alone, until her late husband was laid in the ground. The church minister pleaded with the woman, asking her if she had any instructions for the service, but she refused to talk to him and sat silently in a rocking chair darning socks. When the minister persisted, she flew into a rage and told him: "Do what's to be done and take all the flowers and all the people down there and get you up to the hill and put that old man in the ground. I want my house left in order, too. You tell all those old biddies down there they are to put every rag and tag back in place or they'll every one hear from me, and right soon!"

The stunned minister then stammered that Ward had left instructions for several hymns to be sung at his service, and he asked Willa if the small choir downstairs could carry out the deceased's wishes. This was answered by a blast furnace. "No! No!" she screamed. "By God and by Hell, no! You pray and you mouth your silliness, but you don't turn loose any hymn singing under this roof. Go and finish up down there and then all of you— get out!"

Her angry torrent of words echoed down the stairs, causing open-mouthed gasps. The minister, thoroughly shaken, went down the stairs and conducted the service as quickly as he could, minus the choir singing. Everyone seemed to be in a state of shock. The casket was loaded with restrained haste into the hearse, and people moved out of the house and headed to the cemetery. Annie, Ellie, Marie, and a few others lingered behind a while in the house to help clean things up.

And then a strange thing happened. From the dining room, they heard music. Somehow the ancient gramophone in the corner had turned on, although no one was standing near it. They recognized the refrain: it was "Nearer My God to Thee," Ward Price's most beloved hymn.

Panic struck those still inside. One woman fainted, and others rushed to the front door. The record stopped at the end of the song. The Benson sisters and Marie cautiously moved over to the machine and lifted its top.

There was no record in place on the cylinder!

The sound had not been loud enough to arouse Willa, still upstairs rocking away. The three women were the last to walk out of the house, in stony silence. As they reached the door, they heard it again, "Nearer My God to Thee." Only this time it was much louder. The trio closed the front door, knowing that the now near-deafening sound would surely reach Willa upstairs.

Ward Price, from beyond the grave, was having the last word.

The Vengeful Return of Hetty Cooley

Belle Grove, a magnificent manor house near Middletown, south of Winchester, was built in the 1790s for Major Isaac Hite Jr., a Revolutionary War officer who married President James Madison's sister. It is recorded that Madison called upon his friend Thomas Jefferson to help in the mansion's elegant design.

In 1860, as the clouds of the Civil War were gathering, a bachelor named Benjamin Cooley moved into the house, along with a handful of servants. One of these was a young slave girl, Harriette Robinson, who served a dual role as cook and chief housekeeper. She was feared by others who worked for Cooley because she had a fiery temper, sharp tongue, and totally intimidating manner. She was also strong enough to bully all of the women on the estate, and even some of the men.

After a few months at Belle Grove, Benjamin met a handsome widow named Hetty, married her, and brought her to the plantation to live. Everyone seemed pleased—everyone, that is, except Harriette. She was furious and felt the new mistress would undermine her authority.

Sparks seemed to fly the first time these two dominating women met. In a manner totally uncharacteristic of slave behavior at the time, Harriette openly defied Hetty on virtually ever order she gave her. Things got so bad that Hetty asked her husband to get rid of the hostile servant, but for some reason he didn't.

One day, Harriette stormed into the house and brazenly asked Mrs. Cooley if she had found a stocking. Hetty said no, and Harriette then accused her of purposely hiding the stocking and lying about it. This drove Hetty over the edge, and taking out her pent-up frustrations, she flailed away at the slave with a broomstick. This triggered a wild wrestling match, and Harriette grabbed Hetty by the shoulders and was kicking her senseless when others came in and separated the two.

A few days later, Hetty was sitting in the parlor with her friend Mary Moore, when she got up and went outside. When she hadn't returned hours later, Mary got worried. Then a tenant farmer said that as he walked by the smokehouse, he smelled something strange, like burning wool. A search was conducted, and an old slave said he had heard someone groaning in the smokehouse.

Inside, Hetty was found lying in a semiconscious state, with her feet sticking in a fire. Her face, head, and hair were bloodied and burned almost beyond recognition. Servants carried her to the main house, and a doctor was sought.

After a thorough examination, everyone was appalled at the extent of her injuries. What skin wasn't burned was badly bruised, her right cheekbone was shattered, and her forehead had two deep flesh wounds, laid open to the bone. On her cheek and chin was a clear imprint of human knuckles. It also appeared that she had been choked, as there were fingernail marks on her throat.

When Hetty was asked who had done this, incredibly, she replied that there was nothing the matter with her. She said she had fallen. A few days later, she died without uttering anything else of relevance. Later men found blood all over the smokehouse floor and Hetty's hair under thé door of the adjacent pig room. They theorized that she had not fallen, but had been viciously attacked, and her body had then been dragged from the pig room into the smokehouse.

Harriette Robinson subsequently was charged with the murder of Hetty Cooley. The circumstantial evidence was overwhelming. Several witnesses testified that Harriette had made serious threats on Hetty's life, and the details of their previous fight were brought out. Further, a witness pointed out that the dress Harriette was wearing on the day of the crime was hanging out to dry the next morning after being washed. This was deemed unusual, because she had worn that particular dress for only two days, and normally she didn't change clothes for two or three weeks at a time.

The crowning testimony came from another slave woman, who said Harriette had asked her if she had any poison and told her if she couldn't do anything else, she could poison Hetty. When the woman told Harriette that if she did such a thing, they would surely hang her, she had replied, "I don't care what they do with me afterward. I will have my revenge!"

Completely without any sign of remorse, Harriette was taken to prison and sentenced to hang. She died while incarcerated, however.

It is little wonder, then, that the ghost of Belle Grove is believed to be Hetty Cooley. In the 1870s, only a few years after the tragedy, several members of the household reported seeing the same wispy apparition. As recorded by Marguerite DuPont Lee in *Virginia*

Ghosts, they saw "a white figure standing by the stone fireplace in the basement, then gliding along the flag path to the smokehouse."

Vengeance is sometimes hard to relinquish.

The Protective Phantom Pet

The following incident was reported in newspapers and magazines in the upper Shenandoah Valley and on websites. A soldier identified only as Joe was returning home in 1945 from World War II. When he got off the train, he was still a few miles from his family's farmhouse and had to walk the rest of the distance down a dirt road bordering a river. Eventually he had to cross the river. There were two bridges—one new and unfamiliar to him, the other an old girder type. The newer bridge was closer, so he decided to take it.

Just as he approached it, Joe was met by Shep, the faithful old family dog. He greeted and lovingly hugged the pet. When he got up and started to cross the bridge, Shep suddenly stopped and started barking furiously. The dog tugged at Joe's pant leg and refused to let him continue. Finally Joe decided that for some unexplained reason, Shep did not want him to go that way, so he reluctantly followed the dog to the older bridge.

When Joe reached home, he called out and everyone came running. The family had a joy-filled, tearful reunion. Joe then said, "I would have been here sooner, but Shep made me come the long way." They all got funny looks on their faces and asked him what he meant, so he told them what had happened at the new bridge.

After a long silence, Joe's father told him the news. "Son, Shep died last winter!"

The next morning, Joe learned that the river, raised by heavy spring rains, had flooded the new bridge and swept away the middle section. If he had tried to cross it in the darkness that night, he surely would have been killed.

The Corpse That Rose Up

Waynesboro lawyer J. B. Yount tells of a scary but amusing incident that once happened to his father. The scene was Stonewall Cottage, a family residence outside of Harrisonburg. In 1934, one of Yount's relatives, known as Aunt Laura, died. In those days, everyone gathered at the house instead of the funeral parlor. Several family members and relatives were in the kitchen, reminiscing, when one of the ladies asked Yount's father, then a young man, to go into the parlor, three rooms over, and get her pocketbook.

Yount says his father was never afraid of anything living, but the dead he wasn't so sure of. So as he passed by the coffin in the parlor, he looked down. Aunt Laura was lying in peaceful repose, eyes closed, arms folded. He took another step or two and heard a sharp, loud crack that sounded like a mousetrap snapping. He looked around and saw the dead woman sitting bolt upright in the coffin, her eyes open and staring straight at him!

He froze. Finally, after several minutes of sheer fright, he was able to get back to the kitchen, where he told everyone what he had experienced. The undertaker happened to be there and explained what had happened. Aunt Laura had died at night while sitting upright in a chair, and her body wasn't discovered until the next morning. Partial rigor mortis had set in. So when they prepared her, they wrapped her in a shroud and put a special brace around her neck to keep the upper body in place. Somehow, when Yount's father had walked by the coffin on the creaky wooden floor, the brace had slipped, causing the corpse to rise straight up.

A Voice from the Grave

In the late 1930s and early 1940s, during the latter days of the Great Depression, a number of writers were hired by the Works Progress Administration to fan out across the country and record oral histories. Some of the tales they gathered were folklore legends of years gone by. The following amusing incident was collected by writer John W. Garrett, who interviewed an old-timer named Willie Agee in Alcoma on April 20, 1941. It is recounted here with the permission of the Blue Ridge Institute at Ferrum College, near Rocky Mount.

Agee told of an African American funeral where there was much loud grieving for the deceased. "They had everything fixed up nice. They had a nice casket and the dead man looked good, but it was very hard for the mourners to think about their loved one having to be put in the ground. They said we want pallbearers to be the ones that was his real friends. They had lots of nice flowers, and were paying the last respects to him when it come time for the funeral service. He was taken by the undertaker to the church and the parson gave a very impressive eulogy.

"All of the family and pallbearers was very much touched, there was much weeping, and the assertion was made that 'Oh, if I could only hear brother Paul speak again!' So when the service was over at the church, the funeral procession lined up and the pallbearers followed, with the family behind. It was a large crowd.

"The casket was opened and there was Paul lying all silent in death, ready to be put into the ground. And as the parson concluded the services at the grave, and everyone looked on, someone in the family said again, 'Oh, if I could just hear Paul speak once again!' As the parson was reading the committal and said, 'Ashes to ashes and dust to dust,' the men let the casket drop a bit, and it was such grief to the people.

"So it was that a fellow standing nearby was a ventriloquist. As the casket made the drop, the man threw his voice into the grave and said, 'Don't let me down so hard!'

"Sometime later, one of the pallbearers, who had returned to work, said to his boss, 'You know that Paul spoke out when he was lowered into the ground, and said, "Don't let me down so hard!"'

"'Well,' said the boss, 'what did the people do then?'

"'I don't know,' replied the shaken pallbearer. 'I warn't there!'"

The Figure in White

Lexington historian Charles McFaddin tells a humorous story. About a hundred years ago, an eccentric and egotistical minister named Vanderslice bought some land and built a church on it with his own money. He always dressed in a white suit for his sermons, and whenever he wanted to emphasize a point, he would dramatically raise his right arm high above his head.

When the good reverend died, since it was his own church, he decreed that he be buried under the altar. His wish was carried out, but over time, congregation members swore that on moonlit nights, as they passed by the church in their horse-drawn buggies, they could see the apparition of Vanderslice, standing behind the pulpit with his arm raised, as if he were continuing his fiery oratory from beyond the grave.

It was no laughing matter. In fact, it caused a great amount of fear and consternation. The members were so spooked by the sightings that they decided to build another church just down the street. Several decades later, this newer church fell into decay and eventually was bought and converted into a store. When McFaddin was a boy, his grandfather would drive him up the street by the store and tell him to look through the plate-glass windows as they passed by.

"We would hit a bump in the road, and the car's headlights would flash through the windows, and I swear I saw a white apparitional figure standing in the corner with its right arm raised," McFaddin says. "I had heard the stories, and I really thought it was Reverend Vanderslice. I wondered how that could be."

Years later, McFaddin finally solved the mystery. What he had been seeing was a lifesize model of the Michelin Man, the famous chubby, white figure used by the tire company in its television commercials and newspaper advertisements.

A Quaint Civil War Custom

Having written and published twenty-one books on Virginia's ghosts over the past two and a half decades, I sometimes get strange and curious phone calls, e-mails, and letters. Every once in a while, in sorting through what mostly is a mundane collection of "footsteps in the attic"-type narratives, I find a real gem of paranormal intrigue. A letter I received from Rob Taylor of Arlington in 1998 was just such a find.

"Three years ago, I relocated from New York to New Market, Virginia," he writes. "In a way, moving to the Shenandoah Valley was like a homecoming, since my grandmother was a native Virginian. I started my own computer business, and one of the services I offered was on-site instruction. As a result, I frequently found myself teaching customers who lived in historic old homes.

"I have always been interested in psychic phenomena, so quite often I would ask about the history of such houses, and if it seemed appropriate, whether or not there were any ghosts in residence. Surprisingly, most people said no, but I did come across one interesting incident. Joyce and Frank Winfree of New Market own a lovely stone farmhouse on the edge of town that predates the Civil War. It was built in 1846. I suspected that the house might have served some purpose during the Battle of New Market on May 15, 1864. This was the famous fight in which two hundred raw cadets from the Virginia Military Institute in Lexington heroically took part.

"Joyce told me that, indeed, she had been told by a former owner that the house had been used as a temporary hospital during the battle. But when I inquired about any lingering ghosts, both she and her husband said they had never seen, heard, or felt anything out of the ordinary. Then, almost as an afterthought, she did recall a peculiar experience from several years earlier—one that she and Frank had never come up with a satisfactory explanation for.

"One spring day, they returned from a trip to Harrisonburg and were startled to find the pictures and portraits that normally hang on the downstairs walls were resting on the floor—all of them propped at similar angles against the walls, directly below where they usually were hung. Joyce said the doors of the house had been locked during their absence, and there was no evidence of a forced entry. A cursory review of their valuables found nothing missing, and nothing else out of place. All the same, Frank searched the premises for a possible intruder, but found no one.

"Their next thought was that a minor earthquake or a sonic boom may have knocked the pictures off the walls, but no knick-knacks had teetered off the shelves, and no china had toppled over in the cabinet. And besides, what were the odds that all of the pictures would fall in such a manner, all carefully lined up in order as they were? None were lying facedown, and none had broken glass from a fall. In short, they were mystified.

"Later I called a friend in Pennsylvania and told her about the incident. She too has a fascination with the paranormal. When she heard about it, she immediately recognized the phenomenon. She told me there were several homes in Gettysburg where this periodically occurs, most often in July on the anniversary of one of the great battles there in 1863. It seems that at the onset of a major Civil War conflict, it was a relatively common practice for housewives to remove all of the pictures from the walls of their houses and lower them to the floor, so that the concussion caused by artillery fire wouldn't knock them off the walls in a more violent fashion.

"On my next trip back to visit, I asked Joyce and Frank if they recalled the exact date they had found their pictures lined up on the floor. They weren't absolutely sure, but they thought it might well have been May 15—the anniversary date of the Battle of New Market! It isn't hard to convince oneself that the ghost of a prior resident was taking care to protect the Winfrees' pictures in their absence."

Stone Showers from Hell

One of the most bizarre and celebrated cases of strong paranormal phenomena on record in the United States occurred over a two-year period, ending in 1825. It is considered one of the five greatest cases of poltergeist activity, for which no natural explanation can be given. The events are still talked about today and have been told from generation to generation by descendants of Dr. John McChesney.

McChesney was a physician who lived with his wife and four young children on his farm in a house called Greenwood, about a mile north of the village of Newport in Augusta County, just off the main road leading from Staunton to Lexington. A prosperous man, he owned a number of slaves, among them a twelve-year-old girl named Maria.

It began with her—the first episode that was to lead to total disruption of the peaceful, orderly life at Greenwood. One warm spring afternoon, the quiet was pierced by loud screams from the yard. Maria suddenly burst into the house, obviously terrified, shrieking that an old woman had beaten and chased her. The girl had visible welts and bruises, but a quick search outside revealed no one in sight. The months of misery had begun.

Next, a steady barrage of mud clods and rocks began to be hurled through the house and in the yard. Sometimes they came from inside, other times from the outside, yet no one could determine from where they originated. Often the rocks were hot and actually singed the spots where they fell, and they left sizable dents in the furniture.

Maria seemed to be a special target for the abuse. The girl frequently went into convulsive screaming fits, crying that she was being beaten. The sounds of heavy slaps and blows could be heard distinctly above her cries, and before the eyes of members of the family, great welts appeared on her face and body. While the children found some of these peculiarities amusing and exciting, and Mrs. McChesney was quite upset, the doctor pronounced the whole affair utter nonsense and refused to discuss it or allow anyone to mention it to him.

In succeeding weeks, the volleys of stones continued, thundering down on the roof of the house in broad daylight as well as at night. Sometimes they came thickly, like a barrage of gunfire, but other times they fell singly and hours apart. It was recorded that the stones averaged the size of a man's fist, and some of them were said to be too large to be thrown by a person of ordinary strength. Not once during any of the incidents was anyone seen hurling stones at or inside the house.

Word of the strange and ominous events at Greenwood started to seep through the countryside, and curiosity seekers began arriving. This annoyed Dr. McChesney, who soon abandoned all attempts to be courteous. He drove strangers away the minute he set eyes on them. But still they came. As word continued to spread, hundreds of people from miles around traveled to the farm to see the "Devil's handiwork" for themselves.

Once a group of church elders from one of the nearby towns ventured to the site. They were cordially received and invited to dinner. That evening, as one of them reached for a biscuit, a sharp black rock flew from a corner of the ceiling across the room—and sliced the biscuit in half! It was at this point that a frightened Mrs. McChesney pleaded with her husband to move, but he adamantly refused, contending that no intelligent person could believe for a minute that his home had been invaded by ghosts.

On another occasion, Maria, in a whining, petulant mood, was hanging around the kitchen complaining that she was hungry. Finally she became such a nuisance that the cook shoved her out the door. While the girl stood crying on the back porch, she was pelted with large, floppy objects that appeared to be soggy, oversize pancakes. Servants and members of the family attested to this phenomenon.

During one of the flying-rock episodes, a large rock was thrown into a pitcher with a broad, rounded base and a long, narrow neck that was impossibly small for a rock of that size to have passed through without shattering it. But the rock was there, almost covering the bottom of the pitcher, and there it stayed for many years.

Then the supernatural harassment took a sinister turn. The McChesney baby, James, began to have unusual and frightening seizures. Lying in his crib one day, he suddenly went into a screaming fit, and what appeared to be tiny bloody pinpricks spread rapidly over his body. Mrs. McChesney demanded that something be done, and the doctor reluctantly agreed to send Maria away, to the home of his brother-in-law.

As the slave girl approached the brother-in-law's home, that family heard what sounded like a stampede of horses—inside their house. Rushing in, they found that every stick of furniture and all the knickknacks in the parlor had been piled in the middle of the floor. While they stared in disbelief, clods and rocks began to sail through the room. Panic-stricken, they ran outside and saw Maria. They immediately sent her back to Greenwood.

Following this, the beatings of Maria intensified—night and day, the rocks and clods of mud sailed through the farmhouse and yard—and the baby's seizures grew more frequent. One day, Mrs. McChesney, rocking her son, was badly shaken when a chair against the wall walked across the room and came to rest beside her. Hastily, she moved to the other side of the room, and when the chair followed her, she became hysterical and ran screaming from the house.

Incredibly, Dr. McChesney still could not bring himself to acknowledge that he and his family were up against something evil that defied reason or explanation. He steadfastly refused to leave Greenwood or seek outside help. While the doctor tried, with all his medical skills and knowledge, to cure his son, the seizures increased and James grew weaker. Finally the baby died in the convulsive throes of a screaming fit, while his tiny body flamed with the bloody pinpricks. Only then did the stunned, grieving doctor face the harsh fact that he had so long tried to ignore: some terrible force had been unleashed in their lives.

All of this—the death of her infant son, the continuing blitz of clods and rocks, and the other inexplicable occurrences—was too much for Mrs. McChesney. She told her husband if he wouldn't move, she would leave without him. As a last resort, Dr. McChesney sold Maria and her parents, sending them away forever. From that day on, the mysterious disturbances ceased and never recurred.

The family subsequently moved to Staunton, and the doctor refused, for the rest of his life, to discuss the poltergeist activities.

The whole affair is considered psychically important for a couple of reasons. For one, the family was known as one of respectability and prominence, and they were much embarrassed by the occurrences and reluctant to talk about them. Also, the incidents were eyewitnessed by scores of credible people over an extended period of time.

Were the phenomena caused by the young girl herself? Was she unhappy in her surroundings and venting her wrath by means of psychokinesis? Or were she and the McChesneys being taunted by a vicious spirit who used Maria as the medium for the malicious attacks, avenging some past offense? The deep questions involved here likely never will be satisfactorily answered. But with all the witnesses who said they saw the stones fall, as well as the first-hand testimony of family members and others, no doubt something very strange occurred in Augusta County in the 1820s.

As one McChesney descendant says, "It was real and it was evil, and no one will ever know exactly what it was."

Central Virginia

FROM RICHMOND ACROSS TO CHARLOTTESVILLE AND DOWN TO LYNCH-
burg lie many of Virginia's most cherished sites, including Appomattox Court House, where Robert E. Lee surrendered to U. S. Grant
in 1865, and the state capitol in Richmond, where Thomas Jefferson, Patrick Henry, and others steered the commonwealth through
the Revolutionary War. History oozes across Central Virginia, and
with it the vignettes and anecdotes, the stories and traditions of a
haunted past.

A Scene of Indescribable Horror

It is known throughout Richmond simply as *the* fire. It occurred
the day after Christmas in the year 1811. The site was a theater on
the north side of Broad Street. The occasion was the presentation
of a new play, *The Bleeding Nun*, a comic pantomime. The combi-
nation of the season, the fresh play, and the appearance of a popular actress drew an audience of six hundred, among them some of
the most distinguished citizens of Virginia, including Governor
George Smith.

It happened just after the start of the second act. Backstage, a
young boy was ordered by one of the players to raise a chandelier

of open lighted candles. He pointed out that if he did so, the scenery might catch fire. The player then commanded him in a peremptory manner to hoist the chandelier.

The *Richmond Enquirer* of December 27, 1811, reported the following: "The boy obeyed and the fire was instantly communicated to the scenery. He gave the alarm in the rear of the stage and requested some of the attendants to cut the cords by which these combustible materials were suspended. The person whose duty it was to perform the business became panic struck and sought his own safety. This unfortunately happened at a time when one of the performers was playing near the orchestra, and the greatest part of the stage, with its horrid danger, was obscured from the audience by a curtain.

"The flames spread with almost the rapidity of lightning, and the fire falling from the ceiling upon the performer was the first notice which the people had of the danger. Even then, many supposed it was part of the play. At this juncture, a man stepped out on the stage, and in 'unutterable distress,' waved his hand to the ceiling and announced, 'The house is on fire!'

"The cry of 'fire, fire' passed with electric velocity through the house; everyone flew from their seats to gain the lobbies and stairs. The scene baffles all description. The most heart-piercing cries pervaded the house. 'Save me, save me.' Wives asking for their husbands; females and children shrieking, while the gathering element came rolling on its curling flames and columns of smoke, threatening to devour every human being in the building. Many were trod underfoot; several were thrown back from the windows, from which they were struggling to leap. The stairways were immediately blocked up; the throng was so great that many were raised several feet over the heads of the rest; the smoke threatened an instant suffocation. Many leaped from the windows of the first story and were saved; children and females, and men of all descriptions were seen to precipitate themselves on the ground below, with broken legs and thighs, and hideous contusions.

"The fire flew with rapidity almost beyond example. Within ten minutes after it caught, the whole house was wrapped in flames. In all, 72 people perished in the fire, including the governor, and countless others were badly burned. The aftermath was total shock."

The *Enquirer* later added: "The morning sun rose over the ashes of the chief executive of the commonwealth, and the highest and lowest of the people mingled in an indistinguishable smouldering mass. The holy season for joy and gladness was, to the awe struck community, one of lamentation and of weeping, of deep and bitter sorrow. The state, indeed the whole country, mourned in sincere sympathy with afflicted Richmond."

On the Sunday after the fire, the remains of those who had died were buried within the area formerly included in the walls of the theater, and subscriptions were started to raise an appropriate monument over the tomb. Its cornerstone was laid just seven months after the fire. Known today as Monumental Church, the building was completed in 1814 and is considered one of the state's major architectural landmarks. The entire structure is ornamented with funereal details and references to the fire. The capitals of two columns feature, as symbols of mourning, upside-down torches, stars, and drapes, surrounded by a flamelike carving on a pediment.

Today visitors can walk down a narrow stairway in the back of the church to the basement, and then across dirt floors to the brick crypt that houses the ashes of those who died in the disaster. It is dark and gloomy, and if ever there were a place with cause for the ghosts of anguished spirits to make themselves known in the form of psychic manifestations, this should be the site. But there is only an ethereal silence. It is as if the victims were appeased at the erection of the impressive tomb that shelters them.

A ghost legend is associated with the tragic fire of 1811, however, although few people have ever heard of it. More than a hundred years went by before an extraordinary narrative came to light. The story had been orally passed down from generation to generation in a well-known Richmond family, and it finally surfaced in 1922 in the form of an unpublished monograph written by Mrs. Nannie Dunlop Werth. Her work has reposed in relative obscurity in the archives of the Virginia Historical Society in Richmond. It is with the appreciated permission of the society that some excerpts from that intriguing document are presented.

Mrs. Werth's grandmother, Mrs. Alexander McRae, told her the story, presumably when she was a young girl. Mrs. McRae had been at the theater on the night of the fire. One of the McRaes' neighbors was Mrs. Patrick Gibson, who had adopted as her ward a young girl named Nancy Green. It was through this girl, who was one day short of her sixteenth birthday on December 26, 1811, the day of the fire, that a singular form of psychic phenomena manifested.

Mrs. Gibson wanted Nancy to attend the play that evening, but for reasons unknown, the girl firmly refused, declaring that she did not want to go. Her objections, Mrs. Werth writes, "were finally overcome when her guardian declared that proper respect for her father demanded her presence.

"During the afternoon before the play Mrs. Gibson sent Nancy to Broad Street to make a purchase. En route, she passed along 8th Street and crossed a ravine, from whence she said a Ghost called her, chanting, 'Nancy, Nancy, Nancy Green, you'll die before you are 16!'"

Mrs. Werth's grandmother was present and heard the girl recount the threat when she came home. Mrs. McRae thought "a psychological depression had resulted, and caused the child to not want to go to the theatre that night. She went nevertheless, along with Mrs. Gibson, Mrs. McRae, and several others."

Only Mrs. McRae and two others in the party escaped. Reports Mrs. Werth: "Mrs. McRae was pacing up and down the aisle of the second balcony, suffocating under a heavy burden of smoke, when she was attracted to a nearby window by a burning fragment that fell from the cornice above. She rushed frantically forward seeking fresh air and leaned out. A man's voice cried, 'Jump. I'll catch you.' Knowing it was certain death to disregard the call, she sprang into strong arms and was saved."

Mrs. Gibson died in the inferno, as did young Nancy Green, who, true to the prophetic words of the ghost she had encountered that afternoon, did not live to see her sixteenth birthday.

The Catastrophe at the Capitol

The sounds are heard only at night. Some say they are but the normal creaks, groans, and wind whistles of an old building. But others, including members of the security force, swear they hear voices— soft, muted voices—sobbing and moaning in the darkened stillness of the Virginia State Capitol Building in Richmond. If the sounds are indeed voices, there is good reason for their anguished cries.

Thomas Jefferson conceived the plan for the capitol, patterning it after the Maison Carrée, a Roman temple built in Nimes, France, in the first century A.D. It was the first public building in the New World constructed in the Classical Revival style of architecture and is the second-oldest working capitol in the United States. It has been in continuous use since October 1788.

"Even in its present unfinished state," wrote a visitor in 1796, "the building is, beyond comparison, the finest, the most noble, and the greatest in all America." Here in the grand rotunda is Virginia's most treasured work of art: a lifesize statue of George Washington carved in Carrara marble by the great French artist Jean Antoine Houdon in 1788. There also are busts of the seven other Virginia-born U.S. presidents, as well as a bronze statue of Robert E. Lee.

Ironically, although the building served as the capitol of the Confederacy from 1861 to 1865, it escaped damage during the Civil War, only to suffer a tragedy of enormous proportions five years later in 1870. That year, the general assembly authorized the governor to appoint a new city council. The council elected Henry Ellyson, publisher of the *Richmond Dispatch* newspaper, as the new mayor. However, George Chahoon, who had been serving as mayor, refused to relinquish his office. The dispute got ugly and eventually wound up in the Virginia Supreme Court of Appeals, which convened to hear the case on the fateful date of April 27, 1870.

Everybody who was anybody in the city jammed into the capitol to hear the proceedings in what was sure to be a landmark decision. Hundreds of participants and spectators shoehorned into the courtroom, on an upper floor, and overflowed the gallery.

Minutes before the court met, there was a loud cracking noise, and then pandemonium. The gallery floor collapsed under the weight of the tremendous crowd, and bricks, iron bars, plaster, planks, furniture, and a mass of people plummeted onto the courtroom floor below. Under the impact of this tremendous amount of debris and humanity, that floor then buckled and gave way, plunging to the ground floor forty feet below.

Scores of people were crushed to death immediately, while others suffocated under the huge cloud of dust from tons of plaster that made it all but impossible to see anything. Many were buried alive under the rubble. The pain and suffering were incalculable, and there were screams, cries, and moans everywhere. The lucky ones ran, walked, or crawled outside and fell gasping to the lawn.

Fire alarms were sounded, and firemen, police, and other rescuers arrived, but it took hours to disentangle the bodies. Survivors were carried out to the lawn, covered with blood and lime dust to the point of being unrecognizable. One eyewitness said they looked more like bloody ghosts than human beings. Carriages, hacks, horse-drawn wagons, and other vehicles were commandeered to convey the injured to hospitals. Every doctor and nurse in Richmond was summoned, and when word of the disaster spread, wives, relatives, and friends rushed to the capitol, adding to the anguish and chaos. Some did not learn of their loved ones' fate for days.

In all, sixty-two men lost their lives. More than 250 were injured, some dreadfully, their bodies mangled and their bones crushed. The victims included many prominent citizens, among them Patrick Henry's grandson and several well-known lawyers. Fortunately, the House of Delegates was not in session, or the list of casualties would have been even greater. A curious twist of fate spared the members of the Supreme Court. The proceedings were delayed for fifteen minutes as the judges conferred over some late changes in the written opinion of the case. They were just starting into the courtroom from an adjoining conference room when the gallery floor gave way, and they stood on the very brink of the awful abyss.

Richmond was plunged into municipal mourning, just five years after the city had been sacked and burned by Union soldiers at the end of the Civil War. Business houses closed, and crepe was displayed widely. Resolutions were introduced in the Senate calling for the demolition of the capitol and the building of a new one, but it finally was decided to strengthen and rebuild the existing structure. Ellyson eventually was declared the rightful mayor, and Chahoon later was sent to prison on forgery charges.

Although more than a century and a quarter have passed, and the tragedy is but a black-bordered footnote in history, numerous witnesses over the years have said that the eerie cries and mournful voices, muted under tons of debris, can still be heard in the hallowed corridors of the capitol.

The Ghost with the Tortoiseshell Comb

Many who study paranormal phenomena believe that one reason dead people return to earth in spirit form is because they left something important undone in life. Perhaps they failed to write a will or left before a family dispute was settled. Here is a case that tends to enforce such a theory.

It was first disclosed by Virginia Hawes, who, under the pen name of Marion Harland, wrote a number of successful novels a century or so ago. In her 1910 autobiography, *The Story of My Life*, she told of the phantom woman who haunted the family home on Leigh Street in Richmond for more than thirty years.

One night in the early 1840s, when Hawes was a young teenager, she bade farewell to a visiting guest, locked the front door, and, lamp in hand, started across a small passageway that divided the two first-floor bedrooms. The light shone brightly in this confined area, and she suddenly gasped as she saw, directly in front of her, a small woman dressed in gray "glide noiselessly along the wall," and then disappear at the end of the front hall. The woman was small and lithe, with her head bowed in her hands. She wore a high, carved tortoiseshell comb in her hair.

Years later, Virginia wrote of the occasion: "I have reviewed the moment and its incident a thousand times to persuade myself that the apparition was an optical illusion or a trick of fancy. The 1,001st attempt results as did the first. I shut my eyes to see—always the same figure, the same motion, the same disappearance. She vanished at the front door—the door I had heard myself latch five minutes ago! It did not open to let her through."

At the time, the sighting terrified her. She immediately went to her parents' room and exclaimed, "If there is such a thing as a ghost, I have just seen one!" Startled, her father comforted his daughter and told her to try to sleep. The next morning, he called her aside and asked her to keep what she had seen to herself. Odd, she thought. About a month later, she and her father were in the dressing room one evening, talking, when her mother came in excited and announced, "I have just seen Virginia's ghost. I saw it in the same place and it went in the same direction."

Young Virginia could see that the revelation had shocked her father, but he gathered himself and asked them not to speak of the incident again. They abided. But while they remained quiet, the ghost did not. Virginia's younger sister, Mea, burst into the drawing room at twilight one evening, trembling badly, and proclaimed that something had chased her down the stairs. She said whoever or whatever it was had been in high-heeled shoes that tapped loudly as she descended from the upper chamber. Still, Mr. Hawes insisted that no one talk of the occurrences.

Next, Virginia's fourteen-year-old sister, Alice, and a cousin visiting the house encountered the phenomenon. In the hall one night, they stared, transfixed, as they both saw a white figure moving down the stairs. It evaporated before their eyes. Alice said it didn't go backward or forward; it just dematerialized. The girls screamed in unison, arousing everyone in the house.

The next morning, Mr. Hawes called the family together and told them: "It is useless to try to hide from ourselves any longer that there is something wrong with this house. I have known it for a year or more. One windy November night I had gone to bed as usual before your mother. I lay with closed eyes listening to wind and rain, when somebody touched my feet. Hands were laid lightly upon them, were lifted, and laid in the same way on my knees, and so on until they lay more heavily upon my chest, and I felt someone was looking in my face. Up to that moment I had not a doubt but that it was your mother arranging the covers to keep out draughts. I opened my eyes to thank her. She was not there!

"I have never spoken of this event to your mother until this moment. But it has happened to me not twenty, but fifty times or more. It is always the same thing. The hands, I have settled in my mind, are those of a small woman. Sometimes the hands rest on my chest a whole minute. Something looks into my face, and is gone."

Looking at Virginia, Mr. Hawes said, "You can see, my daughter, why I was not incredulous when you brought your ghost upon the scene. I have been on the lookout for further manifestations. By all means, do not let the servants hear of this. The value of this property would be destroyed were this story to creep abroad. Better burn the house down than attempt to sell it at any time within the next fifty years with a ghost story tagged to it."

Everyone dutifully pledged to remain silent, including, apparently, the ghost—at least for a while. But it resurfaced once more, some time later, this time with comical overtones. That was when a distant relative, described as a "sanctimonious uncle-in-law," came for a visit. He usually stayed several days at least; a fact that caused the family some concern, because they were expecting other guests and needed the spare bedroom. To their surprise, however, he abruptly announced on the morning after his arrival that he had to leave immediately.

Later one of the uncle's relatives explained what had happened. She said he had an awful scare the night he was in the Hawes's house. "He declared he was standing at the window looking out into the moonlight in the garden when something came up behind him, took him by the elbow, and turned him clear around! He felt plainly the two hands that grabbed hold of him. He looked under the bed and in the closet. There was no one in the room but himself, and the door was locked. He said he would not sleep in that room again for a thousand dollars!"

And so the strangeness continued for more than thirty years. Neither Virginia nor any other member of her family was ever able to identify the apparition they had seen and felt. No historical tie-in could be found. Later, however, a telling clue was discovered. After the death of Mr. Hawes and the marriages of the sons and daughters, Mrs. Hawes sold the house to St. Paul's Episcopal Church, and it was subsequently converted into an orphanage.

During the construction modifications, workmen dug an areaway near the front door. Four feet down, they unearthed the skeletal remains of a small woman. And under the woman's skull was a richly carved tortoiseshell comb.

There was speculation that the woman had been murdered or at least died under suspicious circumstances. No sign of a coffin or coffin plate was found. Also, there were no known burials in that residential district. This might explain why she reappeared to haunt the Hawes's house. She may have been in a state of perpetual unrest, seeking retribution for whatever evil had befallen her or, not gaining that, determined to expose that evil.

Once her remains were properly interred, the apparition never appeared again.

The Specter at the Governor's Mansion

The Governor's Mansion in Richmond, the construction of which began in 1813, has seemed to mellow with age, as has its acceptance among Virginians. The commonwealth's *Landmarks Register* calls it "an outstanding example of Federal style architecture." Such was not always the case. Certainly, when it was built it was an improvement over the unpretentious four-room wooden structure that had stood at the site housing earlier chief executives. But not long after the new building was completed, a Richmond newspaper declared it was furnished in a style of inferiority "almost discreditable to Virginia." It further called the mansion's exterior "one of the homeliest dwellings in the city." Later a governor's wife added to the criticism by saying, "There were only three antiques in the house—a tin roof, ugly floors, and copper bathtubs!"

In time, however, a number of improvements were made, and the attitude of the public about the mansion has evolved through the decades to become more accepting. After all, four future U.S. presidents—Thomas Jefferson, James Monroe, William Henry Harrison, and John Tyler—plus Patrick Henry, once lived at this location.

But perhaps the most mysterious resident—or more accurately, intruder—at the Governor's Mansion appeared in the form of a beautiful apparitional young lady. She was first encountered in the early 1890s by then-Governor Philip W. McKinney, obviously a highly credible witness.

He came in one hot August afternoon, took his coat off, washed up in a bathroom, and then entered his bedroom, only to be startled by a young woman who was sitting at the bedroom window. He discreetly retreated to his wife's room and asked her who the charming guest was. She replied, "I haven't any guest," whereupon he reentered his bedroom and the lady had vanished. A search of the mansion turned up no clues as to her identity, purpose, or whereabouts.

The spectral woman was seen on one other occasion. According to Officer Robert Toms of the Capitol Police, one of his fellow patrolmen saw a woman standing at the curtains of an upstairs bedroom in an area where no unauthorized guests were allowed. When he walked over to tell her she shouldn't be there, she flatly disappeared before his eyes, leaving the curtains fluttering.

Although these are the only recorded sightings of the wispy visitor, she has more frequently been heard, and at least once felt. "I've heard footsteps more than once, and there wasn't anyone in the house but me," says one mansion security officer. A number of servants have sworn they have heard her walking about in a rustling taffeta gown. Once a butler chased her down a flight of stairs into the basement, where she inexplicably escaped. She has often been heard by security guards as they sat at a table in the kitchen hallway in the basement. Says one officer, "Many a night I've been sitting there when the governor and his wife were away, and I've heard doors slam and someone walking upstairs. I've gone up to look, and all the doors were locked and no one was there."

During the time of Governor Andrew Montague, just after the turn of the twentieth century, Robert Lynch and Dr. Horace Hoskins were staying at the mansion. One night, both were awakened by the unmistakable sound of footsteps in their room, accompanied by the swish of what sounded like a silk skirt. They got up and followed the sound along the corridor and down the hallway below the stairs, where they lost it. And according to a mansion log, the brother of Governor Montague once "chased the ghostly lady down a staircase and into the street."

A curious incident occurred during the tenure of Linwood Holton in 1972 that added to the ghost's credibility. When Hurricane Agnes whipped through Richmond that year, it caused a city-wide power blackout. All was dark—that is, except for a single lightbulb in the lady's stairwell of the mansion. As an eerie sidelight to this episode, Governor Holton later told a reporter that during the blackout, someone or something moved several of the paintings in his bedroom.

Whoever or whatever the presence is, it apparently was real enough to scare one capitol policeman clean out of his job. Officer Toms says this particular officer was in the basement one night when he distinctly felt something touch his face. He was so terrified that he ran out of the house, throwing down his badge along the way, and quit the force. He came back only to collect his last paycheck.

Once during Governor John Dalton's time in office, yet another officer had a hair-raising experience in the basement. He became curious when the family dog barked furiously at a window, the hair on its back raised. As he stepped over to investigate, he felt a frigid chill in the room. He noticed that although it was in the middle of a summer heat wave, and there was no air-conditioning in the basement, the window had frosted over. The curtains were swirling about madly. In a few seconds, the curtains stilled, and the frost on the window disappeared.

Finally, in December 2006, Governor Tim Kaine told of some strange manifestations he had encountered, which he described as "little quirks." He said a telephone in the family's private residence rang at an inconvenient time, almost every week. "We've never seen an apparition, but we kind of chuckle and think that's just part of living here," Kaine said.

He is not the first governor to experience the curious phone calls. Former chief executive Mark Warner and his wife mentioned the ringing phone to the house staff shortly before they moved out. They said the phone on the bedside table would ring for no apparent reason at exactly 11:45 P.M. on a certain night of the week. Governor Kaine said he tried to find out whether something unusual had happened in the mansion's history at that day and hour, but investigating technicians found nothing.

Who is this mischievous spirit lady, and why does she haunt so historic a house?

There is one possible clue—a vague report that a young woman died in a carriage accident after leaving a party at the mansion more than a century ago. If it is her, she apparently has no political leanings, because she has made her presence known over the years no matter who the governor was.

A Governor's Ghost

Does a former governor still haunt the General Hospital in Petersburg? A woman who worked as a laboratory technician at the hospital in the late 1970s tells of the paranormal phenomena she encountered there.

"The lab I worked in was undergoing renovations at the time," she recalls. "I had been working the night shift then for about six years. Occasionally I would hear footsteps, noises, and muffled voices that I couldn't identify, but since this was a hospital, I just thought it was employees walking through the lab or security people checking the area. I worked alone, and if I didn't see anybody, I would chalk it up to my imagination.

"In the early hours of a hot Monday morning in August, I was standing in the chemistry department running some tests, when I caught a movement out of the corner of my eye. I thought someone had come into the lab, and I turned to see who it was.

"I saw this man staring at me. He was dressed in nineteenth-century clothing. I could only see him from the waist up, and there was a cloud or mist swirling around him. I knew immediately that it was not a living person, because I could see the bulletin board through him. He had the most piercing eyes. I was so startled that I closed my eyes and spoke aloud, 'Whoever is in this lab with me, please leave!' When I opened my eyes, the figure was gone. So, too, was I.

"He never appeared again to me, but he made himself known in other ways, such as off-key whistling and creating cold spots. Sometimes I would see movement out of the corner of my eye, and once something stroked the back of my neck. It was very unnerving.

"I decided to do some investigative work. I found out that the hospital had been built on land once owned by William Cameron. He had built a house here during the Civil War siege of Petersburg in 1864. When the hospital was expanded, the house was torn down. The wing that included the laboratory was the only part of the complex that had been constructed over the old house site."

William Cameron was wounded several times during the Civil War and served as assistant adjutant general. He was elected governor of Virginia in 1881.

The laboratory technician concludes: "My research led me to the Siege Museum in Petersburg, where there is a portrait of William Cameron. It is a picture of the man I saw in the lab that night!"

Premonitions of Death

Premonition has been defined as a forewarning, the anticipation of an event without conscious reason. Consider the case of Julia Gardiner Tyler, the wife of John Tyler, tenth president of the United States. She lived with her husband at Sherwood Forest, a plantation in Charles City County, thirty-five miles east of Richmond.

In January 1862, the former chief executive rode to the capital city to attend a conference. Julia was to join him a week later. However, she had a horrifying nightmare in which she envisioned him dying in a large bed with a headboard crowned with a carving of an eagle with its wings outspread. She was so upset at the vividness of her dream that she went at once to Richmond by carriage. She found Tyler perfectly healthy, and he scoffed at his wife's dream.

Incredibly, two days later, he suffered a heart attack at the Exchange Hotel and died in a bed that matched, in precise detail, the one Julia had seen in her dream.

A strikingly similar incident involved Colonel Robert Gamble early in the nineteenth century. He served with distinction in the Revolutionary War and afterward married Catharine Grattan, an Irish lass who was described as a woman of great energy and character. In the 1790s, the couple moved to Richmond. A prosperous businessman, Gamble rode into the city each day to attend to his various interests and returned home to the outskirts of town each evening. This habitual ritual continued for years. Then, on the morning of April 12, 1810, at breakfast, the colonel noticed his wife was depressed. He inquired, and she told him she would very much appreciate it if he didn't go into town that day.

Curious, he asked why. She told him she had dreamed the previous night that if he left the house this day, he would never enter it alive again. The colonel did not take this warning lightly, for his wife seemed to possess what was then known as "second sight." Today it is called psychic sense. Still, being a practical man, he dismissed his fears, mounted his favorite horse, and went into the city.

He bought a paper on the way, and as he was riding through the warehouse section of Richmond, reading it, fate intervened. Someone carelessly tossed a large bundle of buffalo hides out of an upper window, and it landed in front of his horse, causing it to buck suddenly. Gamble was thrown to the ground, and his head struck a large rock. He suffered a brain concussion and died on the spot.

His associates gathered and formed a group to accompany his body home and inform Mrs. Gamble. At the colonel's house, they were astonished to find her dressed in black, seated in the downstairs hall surrounded by frightened servants.

Before any explanation could be offered by the group of men, Mrs. Gamble spoke: "You see," she said, "I begged him not to venture into the city today, for I knew if he did he would never return to this house alive." Then she told them of her dream. "That is why," she added, "when he insisted on going, I went upstairs immediately and put on my best black silk dress in order that I would be suitably attired to receive his corpse when it was brought home."

Another form of premonition concerning the bearing of bad news occurs when a relative or loved one has a vision of a person, often at the precise moment of that person's death. This is sometimes known as a "crisis apparition." It is as if the spirit of a freshly departed person is trying to communicate to the ones closest to him or her.

A classic example of this occurred in Richmond in the late 1840s, and the story has been passed down through the generations, although the exact names and dates have been lost in the sands of time. It concerned a young U.S. Army officer named James who was serving in the Mexican War.

One morning, James's younger brother was awakened from a deep sleep to find the officer standing at the foot of his bed in full uniform. He was surprised to see his older brother, for there had been no word that he was coming home. He asked James when he had gotten back.

James replied with only this cryptic answer: "Major Smith will see you later and tell you all about it." With that, the figure turned, walked through the door, and into the hall. His brother sprang from the bed and ran after him. No one was there. He searched the house and garden, but found nothing.

A few days after that, a Major Smith arrived at the house and informed the family of the young officer's death on the battlefield. He had died at precisely the moment his brother had seen his image!

Bizarre Happenings at Blandford

One of Virginia's most historic buildings, and Petersburg's oldest, is Blandford Church on South Crater Road. Described by authors James Scott and Edward Wyatt as being "the most precious of all city heirlooms," it was first used in 1737. Next door is Blandford Cemetery, where the veterans of six wars, including thirty thousand Confederate soldiers from the Civil War, are buried.

When the famous Battle of the Crater took place here during the Federal siege of the city in 1864–65, shells riddled the sacred graveyard, causing some bodies to be interred elsewhere temporarily and damaging a number of tombstones. The remnants of the brick wall that surrounds the church clearly show the storm of shot and shell that swept the region.

Perhaps for these reasons, the grounds here are reputed to be haunted. Each Halloween, a bus tour makes a stop at Blandford, and visitors are told of some strange events that have taken place over the years. At least two duels in the early 1800s are known to have been fought on the property. And in the cemetery is the grave of a Corsican named Antommatti, who shot and killed himself in the church long ago because of unrequited love. The church's Tiffany windows are said to soothe his spirit.

One certainly would have sufficient reason to suspect that the ghosts of scores of Civil War soldiers might roam through the hallowed area at night. At least twenty-eight thousand of those buried here lie in unmarked graves. As author M. Clifford Harrison phrases it, "Their names will only be known at the Resurrection, in hope of which they now rest."

Perhaps the most singular paranormal episode at Blandford—one that has never been satisfactorily explained—involves the burial of a man known as Major Jarvis. When he passed away 140-odd years ago, his wife did a curious thing: she left his grave unfilled. That is, she left his glass-topped coffin in the grave uncovered. The story is that when she went to the cemetery to visit, she wanted to see her deceased husband in repose.

Sometime later, she remarried, and no longer feeling the need to view the major, she enclosed the open tomb with a thick marble slab. Apparently the specter of Jarvis took offense, for it is said that this weighty slab would not stay in place. Harrison writes: "At sunset, when the cemetery gates were closed, the slab would appear to be in its proper position. The next morning it would be lying obliquely across a partially open grave. When workmen with crowbars would restore it to its right position and all would seem well, the ponderous slab would persist in slanting again during the ensuing night."

Harrison says he personally experienced the phenomenon. "Once, when walking with a friend at Blandford, I mentioned the legend of the hollow tomb. We walked to the Jarvis Square and paused outside the iron fence. Suddenly, we heard a loud metallic clink down in the grave. We looked at each other with queer expressions on our faces.

"We felt the story of the hollow grave was confirmed."

The Boy in the Picture

Civil War reenactor Jonathan Beckley of the 9th Virginia Infantry was participating in a living-history demonstration at the historic Exchange Hotel in Gordonsville in August 1995 when he witnessed a curious incident take place. A young boy was eating some candy when, out of nowhere, he was approached by what appeared to be a lad about eleven or twelve years old. This boy was dressed in what looked like a genuine Confederate uniform, and Beckley says he was pale, gaunt, and tired looking.

He stared longingly at the boy's candy, and then said he would trade a picture of himself for a piece. The other boy agreed, gave him some candy, and took the picture. Then, suddenly, the boy in the uniform vanished.

The somewhat startled youngster then looked at the picture. It appeared to be an authentic 1860s-era daguerreotype of the boy wearing his uniform.

The Last March of Robert E. Lee

The first nine days of April 1865 were some of the saddest ones in Virginia history. It was during this time that the proud Army of Northern Virginia, under the brilliant command of revered General Robert E. Lee, was driven out of Petersburg after a months-long siege. The men were force-marched across the central part of the state in a last-ditch effort to head south and join the forces of General Joseph E. Johnston in North Carolina.

Outnumbered by more than two to one, half starved and exhausted beyond human endurance, Lee's men nevertheless trudged westward in an attempt to reach railroad lines before the Yankees could destroy the tracks. But their hopes of uniting with Johnston were all but fatally dashed when the Confederates suffered a terrible defeat at the Battle of Five Forks. Then news came that the capital city of Richmond had fallen, and Northern general U. S. Grant's troops were pressing in on all sides.

"No march was as sad as this one," a historian wrote. Still, Lee felt that if he could reach the Amelia Court House, where he had ordered rations to be sent, he could then either turn south or possibly move on westward toward Lynchburg. But it was not to be. When Lee's thirty thousand men reached Amelia, not a single ration was to be found. Lee was devastated.

On April 6, 1865, the Confederates fought heroically at Sailor's Creek, but they were cut to pieces by Northern artillery. Even then, however, Lee moved on to the west in a drizzling rain with his famished and worn-out soldiers. But when the superior Union forces got to Appomattox Court House ahead of him, he realized the end had come. "There is nothing left for me to do but to go and see General Grant," Lee said, "and I would rather die a thousand deaths." On April 9, he mounted his horse, Traveler, and rode off to surrender at the McLean House in Appomattox Court House.

To all who took part in or witnessed that final march during the first nine days of April 1865, it was a tragic and sad event. But was it, in fact, Lee's last march? Perhaps not. At least one eyewitness account says that Lee's battered army marched through adjacent Nottoway County on its final journey at least once more—sixty years later.

This intriguing legend is told by James R. Furqueron, a former director of the Edgar Allan Poe Museum in Richmond, and is recounted here with his permission.

"During the many pleasant summers I spent on my grandfather's farm near Burkeville in Nottoway County," he says, "the most memorable were those evenings when I was permitted to stay up and listen to the elders talk on the front porch. To me, a young lad of nine, this was a high honor indeed. Tobacco farming then was mighty hard work, and the cool of the evening, coupled with appropriate beverages, would put the elders in an expansive and reflective mood. Talk generally centered on crops, the weather, or the damn fool politicians.

"One evening in August 1957, my grandfather was joined by an elderly farmer, then about eighty years old, and others. That evening, the conversation moved from farming to the supernatural. It was then that the old farmer, known throughout the county for his veracity, told of the following encounter.

'It was in April 1925. We was working a farm near Deatonville. I was up in the fields afore light. The sky was jest beginning to lighten a bit, and it was as quiet as a tomb. I never heard nothing, but you know how it is when you think you are being looked at? Well, I turned around and looked up at the crest of a hill, and I seen this fellow on a horse up there. I couldn't make him out real plain, but he was pictured up against the sky and was wearing a gray uniform. Of course, it warn't unusual to see a mounted man that early, but something about this fellow made me right uneasy. He just sat on his horse, the two as still as a statue. It struck me as right peculiar that neither the man nor the horse made any sound whatsoever. And then another thing hit me. The horse's hooves didn't appear to be on the ground!

'Well, sir, after a minute or two, the man raised his left arm and pointed to the west. Then he reined his horse and moved back over the rise, outta sight. All that time I never heared one sound. I'll tell you, I was pretty skeered good, but I reckon I was even more curious. So I walked up the rise and looked out onto the road down below where I figure the feller had gone to.

'There ain't no way for to describe what I seen,' the old farmer continued. 'Going up that road a-heading west, and filling it as far as the eye could see, was row after row of soldiers a-marching, and guns and caissons with men sitting on top! And I seen the flags in that dim light. Lord, they was our flags—the crossed red battle flags of the Confederate Army!

'It was still not yet full light, but I seen 'em, thousands of men and horses and wagons a-moving up that road. I was not more than fifty feet away, and I never did hear one sound! I knowed what it was when I seed it. It was the passing of the dead!'"

Furqueron said the farmer reported seeing this march of the spirit soldiers on April 6, 1925—exactly sixty years to the day Robert E. Lee and his Army of Northern Virginia moved through the same valley on their way to Appomattox.

The Ghost Train at Lomax Crossing

One of the most fascinating cases involving the sighting of a ghost train, engine and all, was recorded in 1985 by Kay Ragland Boyd, who lives near Crewe. Her grandfather was a railroad man and often told her tales of the yard when she was a young girl. This particular account, first published in the *Crewe-Burkeville Journal,* was told to her as an unexplained incident that occurred late in the nineteenth century. It is recounted here with Kay's kind permission.

"The early spring night was cool with a thin crescent moon low on the horizon. Above the single track of the Southside Railway, a plume of black smoke showed darker than the star-patterned sky. At intervals, the lonesome whistle of a steam engine cut through the stillness of Nottoway County.

"The westbound train, part passenger, part freight, thundered by the sleeping village. In the after-midnight silence, the melody of the whistle indicated its passing Cherry Tree Crossing; another two long, two short blasts signaled the train's approach to Lomax Crossing. And then a roar, a crash, an outpouring of steam, a flash of fire, and screams that tore the night to shreds.

"In the latter third of the 19th century, train accidents were frequently followed by the horror of fire which fed on wooden furnishings. Equipment and oil lamps were used for passenger coach illumination. On this occasion, the engine and all five cars derailed, all but the last car crashing down a high embankment west of Lomax Crossing. The town of Crewe was not yet in existence, and how and when help arrived is not known.

"A number of passengers were seriously injured and the engineer and fireman killed in the accident. It was presumed that a 'hot journal box' was the cause of the train's derailing. Whatever the reason, however, a short time later, after repairs were effected and service resumed over that stretch of railway, strange things began in the vicinity of Rodgers' Bank and Lomax Crossing.

"A farmer and his wife, returning from Blackstone, approached Lomax Crossing shortly after midnight a few weeks later. Both saw a train coming toward them from the direction of Nottoway Courthouse. Its approach was silent; no harmonious whistle of the locomotive rent the air, although its headlight was visible, and as they waited for the engine and five cars to pass, the couple saw lights gleaming in the two passenger coaches. After the last car had passed, the flickering red taillights disappeared up the track to the west. The farmer's horse, usually a tractable, easily controlled animal, snorted with terror and shied violently. When finally quieted, the creature had to be led across the track by hand.

"Not long thereafter another strange incident took place in the same locality. The engine crew of an eastbound freight saw what appeared to be the headlamp of a train coming at them from the opposite direction on the then single track line. As the fireman shouted 'Head on!' the engineer set his brakes, believing the proximity of the other train would result in a collision momentarily. Both men were aware of a fleeting, penetrating chill—but there was no collision!

"On looking down the track they saw nothing. The rails, faintly visible ahead of their engine, were clear of all obstructions. As the train moved on toward its destination, the fireman said in an awed tone to the engineer, 'I guess we've seen the ghost train we've been hearing about'; to which the engineer replied, 'I thought we were goners for sure. I hope we never see it again.' The fireman abruptly resigned from the company and the engineer requested and obtained a transfer.

"Next, the owner of a plantation some three miles southwest of Lomax Crossing had spent the day with friends at Locust Grove. He had heard tales of the mysterious phantom train, but had laughed at some folks' imaginations running away with them. He soon changed his mind. As his buggy approached the track on his return home that night, he saw the headlight of a westbound train approaching. He whipped up his horse and made for the crossing to pass over the track ahead of the train. One of the front wheels of the buggy caught in the rail, placing both himself and his horse in what he considered to be imminent danger.

"When his frantic efforts to free the wheel failed, with the headlight moving inexorably closer, he ran a safe distance, abandoning his horse and vehicle to their fate. The planter saw an engine and five cars reach Lomax Crossing, pass harmlessly through his stalled rig, and disappear up the track toward Rodgers' Bank. The horse, completely uninjured but wild with fright, bolted, freeing the buggy, and went off at a mad pace toward home. The man, shaken and thoroughly bewildered by the strange encounter with the spectral train, was obliged to walk the remaining distance to his residence.

"As the eyewitness accounts of the ghost train escalated, a group of Nottoway County planters and businessmen decided to investigate the matter and to find some explanation. Lomax Crossing was being avoided even in daylight. The party of men formulated a plan.

Three of them went to Cherry Tree Crossing (east) and several more to Eleven Oaks Crossing (west), while the remainder stationed themselves on both sides of the track at Lomax Crossing. This was done routinely for a week or more from 10 P.M. to 1 A.M., for the sightings had all been in that time frame.

"Their perseverance was rewarded at last. Those at Lomax (a total of seven responsible witnesses) saw the headlight to the east rapidly approaching their position. No sound of locomotive, no rumble of wheels over track, and no whistle accompanied the light. Some admitted to having been aware of the black smoke drifting upward, and all saw illuminated passenger coaches and the dim red lights of the last car as it vanished to the west.

"When the entire group assembled to compare notes, the following facts became known: those stationed at Cherry Tree saw and heard nothing out of the ordinary—no train passed their check point. The men who had waited at Eleven Oaks told the same: no train had come from either direction. Yet the group at Lomax all saw the phantom engine and five cars!

"Sometime later, the Norfolk & Western Railway purchased the line, made extensive repairs and improvements, and rail traffic increased until the spectral train lost its significance in the frequent passage of freight and passenger scheduled runs.

"Is it not possible that the mysterious silent steam engine with its nebulous five cars may yet pass Lomax Crossing in the night, unnoticed by the progress of modern rail travel? Does a ghostly plume of smoke occasionally hang low over the gleaming rails of steel and is it swept away as a four-unit diesel freight thunders down the track at high speed?

"Will anyone ever know?"

The Spirit Hummer of Monticello

What can be said of the grandeur, the magnificence of Monticello, Thomas Jefferson's home just outside of Charlottesville, that has not already been said thousands of times over by the most gifted of writers during the past two centuries? One of the brochures at the Jefferson Visitors Center puts it well: "Often described as one of the country's foremost architectural masterpieces, Monticello remains today as a testimony to its creator's ingenuity and breadth of interests. Located on a mountaintop in Albemarle County, the house commands a view of the rolling Virginia countryside that Jefferson so dearly loved. It is here that he retreated from the pressures of public office."

Jefferson began his complex dwelling in 1770, and worked on it for more than forty years, altering and enlarging it as his tastes developed. And who could paint the scene with more heartfelt exquisiteness than the man himself? In 1786, he penned: "And our own dear Monticello, where has nature spread so rich a mantle under the eye? Mountains, forests, rocks, rivers. With what majesty do we there ride above the storms? How sublime to look down into the workhouse of nature, to see her clouds, hail, snow, rain, thunder, all fabricated at our feet! And the glorious sun, when rising as if out of a distant water, just gilding the tops of the mountains, and giving life to all matter."

Is there ghostly activity at this great historic mansion? One would surely think so. It is said that when Monticello first opened for public tours in the 1920s, the guides were older African Americans whose only pay was tips from the tourists. They figured the better stories they told, the better their tips would be. Consequently, they related tales of Civil War soldiers riding their horses in the house, and of such things as beds levitating up to the ceiling. Unfortunately, none of the stories were substantiated.

Yet privately, there are a few scattered references to mysterious footsteps and other sounds, certain things that are difficult to explain. And some, through inexplicable personal experiences, have come to believe that perhaps there is a psychic presence here.

Certainly one could make a case for the justification of a Jeffersonian reappearance, aside from his eternal love for Monticello. His spirit must have been distraught that his survivors, weighted down in heavy debts, had to sell the plantation in 1831, just five years after he died. He likely would have been further upset that a subsequent owner tried to sell the house to the commonwealth of Virginia, only to have a nephew overturn the will.

Jefferson unquestionably would have felt uncomfortable with all the gossipy publicity that swirled around his alleged affair with a favorite slave, Sally Hemmings, more than two hundred years after the fact. Would such besmirching of his long-unassailable reputation not be sound reason for him to return and clear the air, so to speak?

And then there is the long unpleasantness that clouded his final resting place, down the mountainside west of the house. No one, not even the sage of Monticello himself, could have envisioned the terrible desecrations that were to follow his interment in 1826. Fifty-three years later, his great-grandson, Dr. William Cary Nicholas Randolph, wrote in the *Jefferson Gazette*: "Where it was certain that no creditor would lose aught by Jefferson, his grandson erected a monument over his grave as was designed before his death. Twice has the marble slab over his wife and daughter been removed, and once the granite obelisk over Jefferson's own grave. Now there is not a vestige of the slabs left, and the last obelisk, chipped and battered by so-called relic seekers, is a standing monument to American vandalism."

It was bad enough that armies of tourists were boldly making off with chunks of tombstones, but then, from nowhere, came a movement to have Jefferson's body uprooted and taken north to Washington. The Northern press picked up the idea and favored it strongly. Family descendants had to mount an attack to keep the body at rest at home. Finally, one newspaper, the *New York Mercury*, brought some sensibility to the bizarre situation, saying: "Jefferson's bones have no business in such a place as Washington in 1882 . . . to which the angels must pay few visits indeed. At Monticello, lifted near the sky, and situated amid sylvan glories, there is peace and purity. Mountain ozone is there, instead of the malaria of the Potomac flats, and the effusoria of political corruption. Let Jefferson's bones alone. They are in honest earth, in an honest atmosphere and among honest citizens."

With that, the ill-conceived movement subsided. But the vandals continued defacing the small cemetery for years afterward. Ordinary people with a ghoulish bent squeezed through the iron bars surrounding the graveyard and chipped with hammers and chisels at anything they could find. Those who couldn't wriggle through the bars hired young boys to do their damage.

It wasn't until well into the twentieth century, when the Thomas Jefferson Memorial Foundation began restoring the building and grounds and Monticello became a national shrine, that the vandalism ceased. Only then, as his great-granddaughter Sara Randolph wrote, could Jefferson "sleep amid the scenes of surpassing beauty and grandeur, on that lovely mountainside, surrounded by the graves of his children and grandchildren to the fifth generation. The modesty of the spot is in striking contrast with the celebrity of its dead, and there are few in America of greater historical interest or more deserving of the nation's care."

Again, would not such actions stir the dead? Would it not be fitting for Jefferson to return to answer his caustic critics and scold those who would disturb his gravesite? Or he might just return for the simple reason that in life, he enjoyed so much happiness here.

Perhaps he does!

Some staff members at Monticello say that on occasion, after the mansion has been closed for the day and the tourists have gone, they have heard the distinct sound of a man humming a cheerful tune, but there is no visible living mortal around.

Jefferson's overseer, Edmund Brown, once wrote that Jefferson "was nearly always humming some tune or singing in a low tone to himself!" Perhaps this signifies that the great man is at peace at last.

A Dreadful Dream of Doom

What appears to have been an incredibly vivid psychic vision occurred in dream form to a farmer in rural Buckingham County, south of Charlottesville and west of Richmond, in the early twentieth century. It resulted in a bizarre, precedent-setting episode of paranormal phenomena still well remembered today.

In 1909, two elderly bachelor brothers, T. C. and W. J. Stuart, lived in a simple log cabin in the isolated woods of the county. They were a reclusive pair and were rarely seen. They walked to town only occasionally to replenish their supplies. Little was known of them. Under such circumstances, a rumor about the brothers was fostered and embellished over the years. It was said that they were filthy rich and a treasure was hidden somewhere in the cabin or buried in the yard. But in fact, the opposite was true. They were dirt poor, but the spreading stories continued to flourish with no one to refute them.

Against this backdrop, on the night of April 17, 1909, the Stuarts' nearest neighbor, a farmer, had an extraordinary dream, totally unlike any he had ever experienced. Not only was what he dreamed crystal clear, but he also remembered every minute detail of it. In the dream, the farmer saw three men, two black and one white, sneaking up the road toward the brothers' log cabin. The farmer followed them at a distance in his dream, but he lost sight of them at a turn in the road. He did not see them enter the cabin.

The time sequence of the dream now skipped ahead, and the farmer's next vision was inside the cabin. There, to his horror, he saw the two brothers lying dead on the floor. One lay near the fireplace, one of his hands pointed toward a hole in the floor, and in the hole was a tin box. Papers were scattered about the crude room. The other brother was slumped in a corner with his head crushed.

At this point, the farmer awakened. The dream had been so real that he was badly shaken. He told his wife about it and asked if she had seen the brothers pass by their house recently. She said she hadn't seen them for several days. Unable to fall back asleep, he got up at daybreak and called the sheriff, describing his nightmare in explicit detail. Knowing the farmer to be a serious man not taken to fancy, the sheriff and others came out, and with the farmer proceeded to check on the Stuarts.

As they got to the turn in the road where the farmer had lost sight of the three men in his dream, they found an empty tin box with papers strewn about. They went on to the cabin and were shocked to see that it had been set afire and was still burning. In the court records of the case, published in the *Virginia Review*, was the following gruesome account: "When the neighbors appeared on the scene they found in the still burning building the partially consumed trunks of two human bodies that were identified with reasonable certainty as the remains of the Stuart brothers.

"The smaller of the two skeletons, answering in size to that of W. J. Stuart, was lying near the fireplace, and a physician who examined fragments of the skull discovered a number of lead pellets embedded in the inside of the parietal bone taken from the left side of the skull, which he identified as shot. The witness also testified that the passage of those shot, from one side of a human skull to the other, would cause instant death. The remains of the other brother were found in a corner of the room with the head missing and the neck smooth as though the head had been severed from the body."

The court report added: "The Stuarts were reputed to have had money, and it was generally believed throughout the county that they were murdered and robbed and their home burned to conceal the crime."

The farmer's description of the alleged assailants he had seen in his dream was so precise that it led to the subsequent arrest of the three men. That the farmer had actually seen the perpetrators of the crime in his vision seemed to be substantiated when a seventeen-year-old black boy came forward and declared he had witnessed the murders. At that time, this was the only record of a dream being admitted as evidence in a trial for murder.

In the summer of 1909, a grand jury of the circuit court of Buckingham County returned a joint indictment against the three parties, charging them with the murder of the Stuarts. Each of the defendants elected to be tried separately. The jury failed to agree in the white man's case, but they found one of the black men guilty of murder in the first degree. The judge, however, set aside the verdict as contrary to the law and evidence. After a searching review of the testimony of the alleged eyewitnesses, including a second man who had come forth after the young boy, the judge characterized their statements as being "so incredible as to challenge human belief."

Meanwhile, the second charged black man was picked up at his house one night by a deputy sheriff and his son, even though they showed no warrant. As they headed toward town, according to the court review of the case: "He was set upon by a mob of armed men, who took him from the custody of the deputy sheriff, and, putting a rope around his neck, repeatedly drew him up and over a limb of a tree for the purpose of extorting a confession. Facing what must have appeared to him immediate death at the hands of these lawless people, he stoutly proclaimed his innocence." The mob then released him, and the deputy sheriff, who allegedly had been in on this brutal action, let him go.

Eventually the Virginia Court of Appeals ruled that the three accused men had not been given a fair trial, and they were freed. Or were they? Two of them died soon afterward, supposedly of tuberculosis. The third man went to work in a West Virginia coal mine and was buried alive in an underground fire.

Was it fate or coincidence? Many Buckingham County old-timers are convinced that the Stuart brothers somehow reached out from beyond their graves to avenge their cruel death.

The Devil in the Flour Barrel

A time-honored classic case of ghostly humor was recorded more than forty years ago in a rare, out-of-print booklet, *The Devil in the Old Dominion,* by historian Alfred Percy. In 1802, an aging preacher named Aaron Crabtree was meeting in Amherst County with a wealthy planter, George Moreland Sr., and his son George Jr. Crabtree's purpose was to persuade them to loan him ten acres of rich creek-bottom land for a camp-meeting ground.

Fervent religious revivals, with thunderous declarations of beating back the Devil by emotionally charged ministers, were the rage of the era. Crabtree could envision himself saving thousands of backwoods sinners at an open tent gathering. He was, however, politely but forcefully turned down by the Morelands.

One spring evening soon after, he approached a tavern on a little ridge where two roads crossed. "What a wonderful site for a chapel," he thought. When he mentioned this to the innkeeper, Ira Beaton, though, Beaton bristled, saying the folks thereabouts were not very religious, and it would be bad for his business. Beaton then left on an overnight trip. Later, a beautiful young girl came out to greet the preacher. She was Millie Beaton, Ira's wife. She was only about twenty years old, and Ira had to be at least twice her age.

It was Saturday night, and the tavern was filled with travelers and local farmers. Drinks flowed from the bar. After a while, George Moreland and his son arrived. Crabtree suddenly leaped onto the bar and began preaching. "Watch out for the fires of hell if you don't repent," he shouted. A stunned silence fell across the room as the imbibers looked up in astonishment. "Your time shall come and you shall face the forks in the road. One way leads upward to Glory, and the other into the fiery pit," Crabtree exclaimed. "Which fork will you take? Why the one to the pit with the molten brimstone to burn your livers because you have no church. I hear the devil's wings flapping as he hovers, peeping in the window."

Glaring directly at Moreland, he continued: "You need a camp meeting in the grove down by the creek where thousands may meet with you to ask forgiveness of your sins. You must have it for I see among you are those on the verge of hell. Shame! Repent!" Crabtree thought he was getting through to just a few in the crowd, but then a group of young people arrived for a square dance scheduled for that evening. Fiddles and banjos appeared, hands began clapping, and the impromptu sermon was unceremoniously halted.

The chagrined preacher slipped off the bar and retreated into the vacant parlor next to the taproom. It had a sofa, a deep chair, and a flour barrel off in the corner of the room. Exhausted, Crabtree sank down into the chair, alone. Some time later, he heard the door open. The shadowy figures of a man and woman quietly entered and sat down on the sofa, totally unaware of the preacher's presence in the darkened room.

It was George Moreland Jr. and Millie Beaton, the innkeeper's young wife. He was pleading with Millie for her to leave her husband and run away with him. They embraced and kissed. Just then the music in the other room stopped, and Crabtree and the couple heard the revelers greeting Ira Beaton. The innkeeper's meeting had been canceled, and he had arrived back at the tavern totally unexpected. Moreland and Millie froze in fear. Thinking quickly, she told her lover to hide in the flour barrel, for Ira would surely enter the room in a minute or two to hang up his coat. Moreland did as he was told.

Crabtree then stood up, and Millie saw him for the first time. Then the door burst open and Ira entered. She rushed to her husband and told him she had been showing the parson the parlor. Suddenly a light flashed in Crabtree's mind. Maybe he could get his campground after all. He would hold the secret of the two lovers over young Moreland's father. He would threaten to expose the couple otherwise. He hated the thought of such blackmail, but he reasoned with himself that the Lord sometimes moved in mysterious ways.

But then at the last minute, he had a change of heart. He couldn't go through with it. He would have to expose the mortal sin he had just witnessed. His dream of the campground would be lost, but otherwise he wouldn't be able to live with himself. As the mob from the other room closed in to get a view of what was going on in the parlor, Crabtree seized the moment. He told Ira the room was full of sin, and to prove it, he was going over to the flour barrel, where he said the Devil himself was hiding.

He snatched off the lid. As Percy writes: "A ghastly, wild-eyed creature, covered in white flour, shot out of the barrel as though impelled by springs. The parson hadn't counted on this whited wraith of a human. He paused only for a second, however, before he shouted, 'Satan! Satan! The ghost of evil and sin!'"

As women screamed and fainted and the men stood in awed disbelief, young Moreland ran out of the room through a service door and disappeared into the kitchen. "For Gawd! It's a hant!" declared a startled cook. One man, heavily fortified with drink, swore he saw the albino figure float through the kitchen and glide past the backyard into the woods beyond, where it vanished. The stunned crowd truly believed they had seen a real ghost.

Crabtree, taking full advantage of the situation, offered a prayer. *Everyone* prayed! Several swore off drinking for good on the spot. Then the preacher thanked George Moreland Sr. for lending ten acres of prime creek bottom for a camp-meeting ground. "It's the first step to keep that ghost from taking some human form we might all know," he said. The visibly shaken but quickly comprehending Mr. Moreland not only agreed to lend the land, but offered ten additional acres as well.

Preacher Crabtree smiled, looked upward, clasped his hands together, and said, "Praise the Lord!"

South and Southwest

Virginia

THE GREAT SOUTHWESTERN TOE OF VIRGINIA IS WHERE THE RESTLESS settlers crossed the mountains in the eighteenth century, fought Indians, and carved out farms from the forests, hollows, and hillsides. They were a hardy band of survivors, who carried with them the beliefs and superstitions of their ancestors from the Old World. Among these were stories of witches and ghosts, a great number of which were preserved by Works Progress Administration writers during the Great Depression. Here, from Roanoke down to the Cumberland Gap, and east across to Danville, South Boston, and Emporia, these legends are still told today.

The Ghost Hound of the Blue Ridge

Sir Arthur Conan Doyle's classic book *The Hound of the Baskervilles* serves as an eerie backdrop to an account of a massive black spectral dog that was reported to have roamed along a certain pass in the Blue Ridge Mountains, southwest of Charlottesville, in the late seventeenth century. A number of book anthologies and newspaper and magazine articles have written about this ghost dog over the past three centuries.

A pass in Botetourt County was much traveled by people going to Bedford County and by visitors to mineral springs in the area. In 1683, news began spreading that at the widest part of the trail, a giant black dog appeared each evening at sunset. The beast walked down the trail about fifty yards or so, and then turned and walked back, as if it were standing guard over something. This would go on all night, and then, mysteriously, the dog would vanish at sunrise the next morning.

Word of this unusual phenomenon spread quickly from one end of the state to the other, and hundreds of Virginians, some traveling great distances, came in hopes of witnessing the event. Many were said to have seen the dog. One particular group of young men mounted their horses one evening and headed for the haunted mountain pass. They encountered what they described as the largest dog they had ever seen. When they approached it, however, their horses snorted with fear and refused to move despite being whipped and spurred.

The dog, meanwhile, marched on, back and forth, as serenely as if no one were there. The men were unable to force their steeds to move along the trail until the dog disappeared the next morning. They decided to return the next night, kill the animal, and bring in its hide. When it appeared at dusk, they fired bullets at it from close range, but the dog kept walking. The bullets had gone right through it and kicked up dust on the ground. The terrified men fled.

The ritual continued, night after night. Then one year, a beautiful woman from England arrived in the area. She was looking for her husband, who had preceded her to America and said he would send for her when he got settled. She had not heard from him again and crossed the ocean to search for him. She traced him to Bedford County, but there the clues ran out. Then she heard the story of the ghost dog and said she and her husband had owned a dog like the one described.

She asked if some men would lead her to the site where the dog appeared each night. That evening, at sunset, the dog materialized as usual, but instead of walking down the trail as it normally did, it went straight to the lady, laid its head in her lap, and moaned. Then it started up the trail, looked back to make sure she was following it, and led her to a spot where it paused by a large rock. It pawed the ground, gave a long, low wail—and evaporated.

The lady asked the men who had traveled with her to dig at the site. When they dug below the surface, in a shallow grave, they found the bones of a very large dog and, beneath them, the remains of a human skeleton. There, on one of its bony fingers, was a signet ring that the lady identified as her husband's.

She had the bones properly buried and returned to her homeland. And the ghost dog, having completed its faithful vigil, was never seen again.

Bertha's Bouncing Bed

Deep in the mountains of Southwest Virginia, the folklore legends of generations and centuries ago are so well entrenched that sometimes today it is difficult to separate fact from fiction. One such tale, still told with relish and delight, is that of "Bertha's Bouncing Bed." This psychic phenomenon, which occurred over an extended period of time, was witnessed by hundreds of people from miles around, including a number of so-called experts and several newspaper reporters.

One of the more definitive accounts of the activity was recorded in 1938 by I. M. Warren as part of the Virginia Writers' Project during the last years of the Great Depression. In his travels, Warren tracked down the origins of the bouncing bed legend. The site was on the north side of Powell's Mountain in Lee County, about eight miles from Jonesville, the county seat. Here, in a small, three-room log cabin, lived Robert Sybert and his wife, Rebecca Jane.

They had moved to this isolated, hilly, and desolate section of Virginia in the 1880s from Missouri, bringing their household furniture with them, including what was to become the infamous bed. The couple had one married son, Robert, who lived near them. He had a son and three daughters. The oldest girl, Bertha Marie, was nine years old at the time. She was small and slender and was said to have a bright mind.

According to Warren: "The peculiar occurrence consisted of a shaking movement of the bed in which the child slept. So persistent became the sketchy tales of the quivering, quaking bed, and accompanying uncanny scratching noises, that area citizens of substance, usually quick to dismiss weird accounts from the backwoods that smacked of the supernatural, began to take this account seriously."

The Syberts, grandparents of Bertha, welcomed a delegation of witnesses to their humble home on December 18, 1938, and invited them to see for themselves. Mrs. Sybert, then seventy-one, told those present that she had lived in the cabin since 1888 and had given scant attention to unusual incidents that defy logic.

"Four weeks ago," she said, "Bertha began to hear unusual noises, just as if someone were rasping a nail across the head of the old wooden bed in the corner. The noise continued for several nights, until the bed where the child slept began to quiver. This week it's been so bad that Bertha's bed bounces and shakes something awful. You can stand across the room and see it as plain as day."

The delegation was not disappointed that evening. "Sure enough," one witness exclaimed, "it began shortly after six o'clock. The bed quivered and trembled, yet the house was steady." A Baptist minister present commented, "I saw the trembling bed, but such things are just beyond my knowledge."

Warren reports that the nocturnal quakings did not seem to be confined to the old wooden bed, but occurred in any bed the girl slept in. At one point, Grandmother Sybert said, "It must be witchery, because the old bed makes me sore through my back when I get in bed with Bertha. It upsets me, too." Once a Bible was placed under the bed and all was quiet. With that one exception, the bed had bounced every night for a month.

Thousands of people came to the little cabin during December 1938, after a Bristol radio station aired the strange scratching sounds over the air. Writes Warren: "A curious throng waded ankle deep through mud and driving rain and sleet on the night of December 23, in hopes of seeing the 'capricious ghost.' Ghost or witchery is the family's answer to the weird quivering of Bertha's bed. Neighbors and visitors, after repeated visits to watch the child jostled about, haven't offered anything more tangible to hang an explanation on."

Finally, two psychology professors from the University of Tennessee came to investigate. The saw the bed gyrate and heard the scratching noises. Astoundingly, they dismissed the incidents as pure fakery. "We have no doubt," they wrote in a report, "that the child makes conscious, deliberate contractions of the buttocks which explains the peculiar swaying of the mattress. The squeakings and scratching are the result of the dilapidated condition of the spring and bedstead. The darkness of the room helps conceal much."

Instead of laying the issue to rest, however, the professors' report stirred up a fury. Scores of credible witnesses said the phenomenon was real, not staged. State Senator John C. Neal of Pennington Gap, for example, who had personally seen the manifestations, dismissed the conclusions of the professors by saying their examination was "lame and incomplete," adding, "The mystery is yet unsolved."

The bed continued to bounce for more than a month, and then, abruptly, it stopped. To this day, however, no one can convince the people of Lee County that the solution of the mystery does not lie somewhere in the netherworld of the paranormal.

Converted by a Ghost

A strikingly similar case was reported by Works Progress Administration writer James Taylor Adams, who collected hundreds of folklore legends throughout Southwest Virginia during the Depression years. On November 18, 1940, Fletcher Sulfridge of Wise County told Adams a strange story of another bed that seemed to be possessed. It is presented here with the permission of the Blue Ridge Institute at Ferrum College in Rocky Mount.

According to Sulfridge, the phenomenon occurred sometime around 1910. A man named Greear lived out in the Flatwoods of the county. "Old man Greear was an unbeliever," Sulfridge said. "He didn't go to meetings and didn't believe in any church. He had a wife and several children. One boy, about fifteen, was an awful good singer, but he took down sick and died, and they buried him in the graveyard up on the point just above the house.

"About a year after the boy died, there was a big revival going on nearby, and Greear's wife and girls all went. He wouldn't go. Stayed at home by himself. They got the preacher to come out one night and talk to him, but it done no good. He said, 'I ain't goin'!' The revival went on. The girls were all saved. Mrs. Greear had been a Christian a long time.

"Well, one night just after the meeting had broke up and they got back home, they were sitting around talking and Mrs. Greear and the girls was pleading with him to go the next night. Suddenly, they heard somebody a-singing. Went like it was up at the graveyard, and sounded just plimeblank [exactly] like the boy that had died. It [the voice] came nearer and nearer till it seemed to be right over the house. Then it stopped and a little light come right through the wall and went under the bed. They looked under the bed but couldn't see anything. But after a while it came out and went right back up the wall, around the ceiling and out through the wall. Then the singing started again and went off up the hill toward the grave-yard. It was exactly ten o'clock when it started.

"Next night they got home earlier than usual and had gone to bed by that time. They heard the singing again, and again it come on down the point and over the house and hushed. Then the light came through the wall and around the ceiling and down the wall and under the bed. And the bed just lifted up and set over in the floor and began to dance about. They jumped out of it and Mr. Greear grabbed it and tried to hold it, but it just throwed him about and kept on jumping about. After awhile the bed moved back to where it had been and the light came out from under it, crept back up the wall around the edge and out through the solid wall. And the singing started off again.

"It got rumored around and the whole neighborhood gathered to see and hear it. The fifth night nearly everybody at the meeting come to see it. It done the same thing. Four of the strongest men they could pick out got one at each corner and tried to hold the bed in place, but they couldn't do it. It just throwed them about same as if they had been dolls. It just kept right on.

"Mr. Greear seemed to be thinking a lot. The sixth night his wife talked him into going to the revival meeting. That night it came again. The seventh night he went, too, and went to the mourner's bench. That night it was just the same thing. The ninth night, he confessed religion, and the singing was not heard or the light seen no more. I don't know what it was or what it was for, but it con-verted old man Greear!"

The Phantom Car Ride

A few years ago, a young man was driving along Route 60 in a heavy rainstorm, heading toward West Virginia. He skidded on the slippery road and ran off into a ditch. He had passed a tavern five miles back and decided to walk there. On his way, he saw a car coming up a steep hill at a very slow rate of speed. When it got to him, it virtually stopped, and he jumped in.

He profusely thanked the driver for allowing him in out of the storm, but he got no response. Then he noticed that the windshield wipers weren't on, though it was still pouring in torrents. He became a little frightened and took out his cigarette lighter and lit it. There was no one behind the wheel! Then, as the car was going around a curve, a bony arm suddenly reached in and steered the car around the bend.

This freaked the young man out, and he jumped out of the car and ran all the way back to the tavern, where he told the people there what had happened. About thirty minutes later, two men arrived, soaked. They looked around, and one of them pointed at the young man and said, "There's the idiot that jumped in our car when we were pushing it up the road!"

The Resurrected Grandmother

Henry County historian Carl DeHart, associated with the Blue Ridge Regional Library, tells of a humorous yet scary event that occurred in 1938 on a dairy farm at the extreme southern end of Virginia. An African American man named "Doc" Smith and his aged grandmother lived here in a two-room log cabin. She was described as wraithlike and had long, white hair down her back. Youngsters in the area referred to her as the ghost woman.

One day in the depth of winter, with five inches of snow on the ground, Doc found his grandmother apparently dead. He could discern no pulse or heartbeat. As was the custom in those days, a "sitting up with the dead" session, a wake, was held. Because they were so poor, there was no casket. The grandmother was laid out on a table in one room with a sheet placed over her. Close friends and relatives gathered to pay their last respects.

As it was freezing cold outside, a fire was going full blast in the fireplace, and all the folks stood or sat in front of it with their backs to the table. Suddenly, without anyone noticing it, the sheet began to flutter, and the "dead" woman sat up. She apparently had lapsed into some sort of deep catatonic coma, and the heat from the fire had revived her.

She slid off the edge of the table, walked over and tapped a man on the shoulder, and said, "Sho is cold out tonight, ain't it?"

As one might well imagine, there was an immediate stampede for the exit. The terrified friends and relatives banged into each other as they headed for the door in a crazed dash. Hysterical screams filled the tiny cabin, and there was a frantic pileup at the door as the men and women clawed at each other in sheer panic trying to get through the narrow opening. One gentleman was so rattled by the old woman's sudden resurrection that he tried desperately to squeeze his body up the chimney!

Haunted Room 403

In the far southwestern corner of the commonwealth lies Abingdon, a town *The Virginia Landmarks Register* says "is unusual for its large quantity of federal and antebellum buildings of brick, which serve to give the district an air of permanence and prosperity lacking in similar settlements containing mostly wooden buildings."

Colonel Francis Preston built one of the largest houses here in the 1830s. This was later converted to the Martha Washington College for girls, and today it is the famous Martha Washington Inn, a four-star, four-diamond hotel adorned with antiques and period furniture. It also is one of Virginia's most haunted places.

Most of the still-active psychic phenomena here date to incidents that occurred during the Civil War. An apparitional horse is said to sometimes roam the grounds on moonlit nights, seeking its rider, a Union officer who was shot down in front of the building in 1864. Then there is the touching saga of a young Confederate soldier who raced into the inn one day to warn of approaching Federal troops. He ran up the spiral stairway just as his pursuers broke down the front door. From the top of the stairs, the story goes, he felled seven men before he was mortally wounded and bled to death in the arms of one of the student nurses.

A prevailing legend has it that his bloodstains can never be washed away and can still be seen beneath the carpet. "It's a strange thing about that spot in the carpet," says Pete Sheffey, a bellman who has worked at the hotel for more than forty years. Every time new carpet was put down, it seemed as though a hole would somehow appear where the young Confederate had fallen. "I can remember my grandfather talking about it back in the 1930s," Pete says. "He saw the bloodstains then, and he said every time they covered it up, a hole would show through at that spot. I think they have replaced the carpet there six or seven times since 1937. No one could ever explain why that happened."

Pete also says many hotel workers have experienced various forms of otherworldly manifestations over the years. "There were old slave quarters here on the grounds, and I've been told that some of the old slaves were buried under the hotel and even in the walls of the old quarters. I don't know if that means anything, but I can tell you a lot of peculiar things have happened here." Pete's grandfather said he once encountered the spirit of a Confederate soldier while walking down a long, darkened corridor one night more than sixty years ago. "He said the man had on a gray uniform, and part of one leg had been shot off."

A number of employees have reported seeing wispy figures floating around. Maids have entered certain rooms and walked into inexplicable icy cold spots, even in the middle of summer when the air-conditioning was off. Others have seen doorknobs turning when no one was outside the door. A housekeeper says she once encountered a "smoky-like object" at 6:30 A.M. as she sat in the lounge. Stunned into silence, she watched as it drifted across the room, headed toward the door, and vanished. Desk clerks have reported seeing a similar figure appear and disappear in the lobby during predawn hours. There also have been sightings of apparitions ascending and descending the stairs, and a female guest screamed one night when she woke up and something was hovering over her bed.

It is an old building, Pete points out. "There are a lot of long hallways and high ceilings and creaking stairs and such. But too many things have happened here to dismiss them all as being the settling sounds of an old hotel. I've seen what I could call 'flashes' myself, like someone or something was passing by and I just caught a sidelong glimpse of it. But when I turned around, there was nothing there."

Of all the eerie episodes at the Martha Washington Inn, however, perhaps none is more intriguing, or more romantic, than the periodic spectral return of a lovely young lady named Beth, who infrequently comes back to Room 403 to care for the handsome young man who died there more than 140 years ago. She was a student at the college in early 1863, a time when part of the school had been turned into a hospital to tend to grievously wounded soldiers.

One of these was John Stoves. He had been brought in one day, shot half full of musket balls, and placed in what is now Room 403. Beth changed his bandages and comforted him as best she could. When Stoves learned that she could play the violin, he asked her to do so. She happily obliged, and although he was suffering from severe pain, her playing seemed to put him at ease. He would fall asleep listening to her. As the young officer slipped ever closer to the "other side," Beth, it is said, fell in love with him.

One day she was summoned to come to the room quickly. Lying near death, Stoves smiled and asked her to play her violin for him. As she did, he closed his eyes and passed on. She clasped his hand and cried. She never got over the shock, and within a few weeks, she too was dead—some said of complications from typhoid fever, others of a broken heart.

Ever since that time, a haunting presence has seemed to envelop Room 403. A security guard at the inn recalls that one night when making his rounds, he passed a "milky-like figure" with long, flowing hair on the stairway. He asked if he could help her. She did not reply. She instead seemed to glide up the stairs, and then she went through the shut door to that room. Maids have told of seeing the wraith of a slim, young girl sitting in a chair by the bed.

And some say that in the late hours of the night, they have sometimes heard the soft wafting refrains of a violin.

The Recurring Wreck of Old 97

A historical marker in Danville reads: "Here, on September 27, 1903, occurred the railroad wreck that inspired the popular ballad, 'The Wreck of Old 97.' The southbound mail express train on the Southern Railroad left the tracks on a trestle and plunged into the ravine below. Nine persons were killed and seven injured, one of the worst train wrecks in Virginia history."

Curiously, there were at least four separate omens of pending ill fate regarding the final, fatal run of Old 97. The first was in its late departure from the depot in Washington, D.C. Northbound mail trains were running behind schedule, and this delayed 97 for an hour, a fact that caused considerable concern, for this crack express train had a prideful reputation of being on time as it raced south through Lynchburg and Danville, heading across the Carolinas to Atlanta.

The second omen centered around the engine itself, locomotive number 1102. A year earlier, her wooden cab had exploded into flames, causing a wild, out-of-control ride until the engineer and fireman were finally able to reenter after the fire had consumed the wooden portion of the cab.

Third, there was much grumbling among the crew members on that fateful morning over part of the train's cargo—a large shipment of live canaries. This did not bode well at all for the superstitious-minded.

And finally, an inexplicable incident occurred when 97 stopped at tiny Monroe, just north of Lynchburg, to change crews. The regular relief crew, for some still unexplained reason, was, at the last minute, transferred to another train. This was a particularly scary omen to railroad old-timers, who believed a strange hand on the throttle was a portent of lurking danger.

That hand belonged to Joseph B. "Steve" Broady. Despite the best efforts of the regular crew, no time had been made up between Washington and Monroe, so it fell to Broady and his team to slice off as much time as they could on the next leg of the run, from Monroe to Spencer, North Carolina. The train, which included the locomotive, two mail cars, and two baggage cars, normally stopped in Lynchburg for several minutes, but on this day, Old 97 stopped and started up again so fast that seventeen-year-old Wentworth Armistead, who had been sent aboard at Lynchburg to check the locks on the safes, didn't have time to get off.

It was now past 1 P.M. The train was due in Danville at 1:40, and there were sixty-four miles still to cover. Broady ran the throttle wide open, slowing only slightly for treacherous curves as the cars threaded through the hills and valleys of southern Virginia. Old 97 was hurtling so fast that passengers complained they had difficulty seeing the countryside.

The train whizzed past junctions at Altavista, Gretna, and Chatham at record speeds—but ultimately at a terrible price. Engineer Broady was, in railroad parlance, "eating steam." He ran full out, shoving his throttle on straight stretches, and pulling the brake valves on curves only enough to permit safe passage. Railroaders called this throttle-brake procedure "whittling," and although it speeds the pace of the train, it has a frightening downside—it consumes steam and air pressure faster than the compressors can produce it. Apparently, while Broady concentrated his attention on the unfamiliar (to him) terrain ahead, he either forgot or ignored the gauge that regulated his braking pressure. He seemed a man hell-bent on making up time at all costs.

And, in fact, Old 97 had made up about half an hour on the whistling run from Lynchburg, as it entered the most perilous portion of its doomed journey, a three-mile, curving downgrade that led to the trestle crossing the Dan River on the outskirts of Danville. At the bottom of this long descent was the most dangerous curve of all, which veered sharply to the east. Below the trestle at this point was a seventy-five-foot sheer drop into a deep chasm over Still House Creek. On each side of the rails north of the curve were ominous warning signs: "Sharp Curve. Speed Limit 15 Miles per Hour!"

Broady approached this treacherous stretch at full speed. Eyewitnesses said that Old 97 was going faster than anything they had ever seen as it hit the three-mile downgrade. Only when he saw the warning signs did Broady shove in his throttle and pull back on the brake lever. To his horror, nothing happened. The air pressure was gone. Frantically, Broady began dumping sand on the tracks and tried to reverse the pistons.

But it was too late. An old magazine article describes what happened: "The engine struck the first rails of the curve, wavered and swayed for a moment, then continued straight ahead. With a sickening lurch, the stampeding locomotive left the track and bounded onto the trestle, bounding and skipping along the crossties while wood splinters flew in every direction. The mail car behind the tender left the rails, then the second car, the third, and the fourth.

"The runaway express rolled to the right, leaped above the yawning chasm, and fell toward the bottom. With a thud and roar never before heard in Danville, the engine's left side struck the creek bed; she half-buried herself in the mud, the drive-wheels continuing to turn slowly. As steam spewed in every direction, the four cars tumbled and shattered almost on top of the overturned locomotive. The last car struck the pile of debris; its wheel bounded off; and it came to rest with one end pointing to the sky, as if gasping for air.

"For a long moment the awful silence of death hovered over the scene. It was soon broken by the frantic shouts of rescuers, and the shrill songs of hundreds of freed canaries flying wildly overhead."

Broady and his two firemen were found near the locomotive cab. They had been scalded almost beyond recognition. Broady's watch was found. It had stopped at 2:18 P.M. Dead, too, was young Wentworth Armistead, who had not had time to get off the train in Lynchburg, and five others, including a new bridegroom. Rescuers dug through the 350 tons of wreckage for a day and a half.

Certainly, any of the crewmen or passengers who died as a result of that omen-fated ride in 1903 would surely have just cause to return in spirit form to the scene, especially young Armistead or a remorseful Steve Broady.

Perhaps they do!

It has been told by Danvillians for more than a century now that if one stands still, on an autumn afternoon at a little past two, at the foot of the three-mile downgrade and listens closely, Old 97 echoes yet through the Valley of the Dan. Scores of witnesses down through the years have attested to this ethereal phenomenon.

A strangely coincidental footnote to the saga was added sixty years later when the following dispatch was filed on September 28, 1963, by United Press International: "Yesterday, at about 1:30 P.M., Robert Burns George, 78, of Gretna, Virginia, was killed by Train Number 21 as it passed through town. Number 21 replaced famed Mail Train 97 on its run from Washington to Atlanta. George, who was walking along the tracks, stumbled in front of the engine.

"He died on the anniversary of the wreck about the time 97 would have passed Gretna, had it still been running." And the eeriest thing of all: he was the nephew of the man who wrote the song "The Wreck of Old 97."

The Little Rag Doll

The origins of the following legend can be traced back to a rural district in Southwest Virginia early in the twentieth century. It has been passed down ever since. A new teacher for the local elementary school had been summoned when the previous teacher, abruptly, unexpectedly, and without a word of explanation, suddenly quit and left the county.

Curiously, the principal told the new young woman that she had to leave the school each afternoon no later than 2:30. Odd, she thought, but she followed the instruction, and everything went smoothly for two months. As Thanksgiving was approaching, however, the teacher became absorbed in making plans for a holiday play and, not noticing the time, stayed past the deadline.

At 3 P.M., she heard an unusual call of a strange bird, and then felt an unearthly chill. The room temperature dropped 30 degrees. The teacher looked up from her desk, and there stood an ashen-faced wraith of a little girl, about eight or nine. She seemed to have appeared out of nowhere. In a faint voice, the girl whispered, "Teacher, what is my homework and where is my rag doll?"

Startled, the woman stood up, and the girl, apparently frightened, ran out of the room, dropping a book on the floor as she did. Instantly the room temperature returned to normal. Curious, the teacher picked up the book. Nearly worn out, it had been published in 1890 and was long out of use. The teacher went to the principal and told her what happened. The older woman seemed angered that her rule of not staying past 2:30 had been broken, but she said nothing else.

That night, the teacher decided to hand-stitch a rag doll in case the girl came back. The next day she purposely stayed late, and the same eerie scene was repeated. She heard the bird call, the temperature in the room plummeted, and the little girl entered the room. She again asked about her homework and her rag doll. The teacher told her to read the first three pages in her book and said, "Here is your doll," handing both items to the girl. Then the girl turned toward the door and simply vanished!

The teacher went back to the office, and this time the principal took her by the arm and said, "Let's take a walk." They went through a patch of woods, and the principal told her that many years ago, a nine-year-old girl went to their school. One day, while playing in a creek after school, she slipped, hit her head on a rock, fell into the icy water, and drowned.

The two women walked a little farther, to a small graveyard, where they saw a tombstone with a tiny angel on top of it. The inscription read:

Emily Caldwell
Born 1902—Died 1911.

A Visit from the Devil

In *Tales from South of the Mountain*, author, historian, and folklore expert Elzie "Sock" Mullins, a native of "The Pound," Wise County, in the far reaches of Southwest Virginia, says the following amusing incident really occurred. Early in the twentieth century, the class of a small rural school decided to hold a masquerade party one Halloween. One seventh-grader dressed in a bright red suit as the Devil. On the night of the occasion, the lad started walking along a two-mile route to the school. About halfway there, a rainstorm came up suddenly, and he looked around for the nearest shelter. He saw a light in a little country church and headed toward it.

Mullins describes what happened next: "It just so happened that the people in the church were in the midst of an old-time revival. The minister was preaching from the Book of Revelation, and solemnly announced that the end of time was near. He said, 'The Lord is going to soon call you, or the devil will be coming after you.' Just then there was a terrific flash of lightning followed by a booming crack of thunder. The front doors of the church suddenly sprang open, and there stood the boy in his devil's costume, horns on his head and pitchfork in his hand!

"Such screaming you never heard before! The preacher made a mad dash for the back door. Out the side windows some of the members went, like scared rats when a weasel invades their den.

"The boy drew back his pitchfork and walked down the aisle. Within a minute everyone had evacuated the building except a lone old crippled man. He turned, facing the boy, and nervously said, 'You know, I've been a member of this congregation for over 30 years—but I've always been on your side!'"

Old Cleveland's Last Ride

Author-historian Gay Neale of Brodnax tells of a supernatural encounter in one of her books, a definitive history of Brunswick County. The following narrative is recounted here with her gracious permission.

"Only once in my life have I seen a ghost. It was not a bad experience at all. Half a mile up my country road lived a man named Grover Cleveland Holmes. I lived here for over a year before I ever saw the man. He was sitting on a flat rock by his mailbox—an old black man, wearing a shapeless gray raincoat, and squashed down on his head was an equally shapeless hat. If I had been going any faster in my truck, I never would have noticed him. I stopped and called out, 'Do you need a ride?'

"'Don't need one, ma'm,' he answered, 'but I'll take one if it come, and it always do.' Cleveland climbed into the truck. He smelled discreetly of liquor, and he preached all the way to town. He apparently was a deeply religious man. When we got there he asked me what he owed, and I said not a thing. I had enjoyed the ride. 'Hey, wait a minute,' I said. 'How are you going to get home?' 'Oh, I speck someone be going my way and they'll take me along.' I felt good all day.

"Quite often over the next few years, I gave old Cleveland a ride into town. I would slow down past his little house and check the big flat stone. If he were there, he'd slowly climb in and start preaching. He always got home, too. Someone always seemed to be going his way.

"One fall he rode less often. I knew his cousin and she told me he was 85 years old and a veteran of World War I. That winter was a cold, dreary one. I didn't see Cleveland for a long time. His cousin told me he had fallen asleep one night and let the fire go out and his feet froze. They had to amputate them. And so, for many months, I didn't slow down when I passed by his house. I missed him and his homespun sermons.

"Then one day I was driving a little too fast down the road. As I passed by Cleveland's house, I saw, from the corner of my eye, a figure hunched over by the big rock. Gray raincoat, shapeless gray hat. I slammed on the brakes and whirled around to look back . . . but there was nothing there! That had been Cleveland, by gum, plain as day!

"When I passed by Cleveland's place on the way home that day, I saw a sprig of plastic flowers that the undertaker sticks on the house of someone who had just died. I felt something turn over in my stomach. I called his cousin. 'The gangrene got him,' she said. 'They couldn't stop it.'

"So I figure I saw old Cleveland waiting there for someone to be going his way—and sure enough, they were—and they took him along!"

Tidewater
Virginia

ON THE SHORES OF THE CHESAPEAKE BAY AND THE ATLANTIC OCEAN, stretching from the Northern Neck and Tappahannock down to Newport News, Hampton, Norfolk, and Virginia Beach, is Tidewater Virginia. This region includes Jamestown Island, where the first settlers landed in 1607; the restored Colonial Williamsburg; and the coastal communities, where watermen have plied their time-honored trade for centuries. And here also, preserved along the rivers, waterways, and wetlands, are accounts of the supernatural, including the legendary accused witch Grace Sherwood and the alleged spectral return of such famous men as Jefferson, who once walked the streets of Williamsburg, and Lincoln, who helped plan Civil War strategy at historic Fort Monroe in Hampton Roads.

Tragic Teardrops in the Snow

It's a story unmatched even by Edgar Allan Poe's most imaginative fictional narratives. The setting is Church Hill in Gloucester, where a large frame house still stands today on an elevation just above the Ware River. The property passed in a direct line to descendants named Throckmorton. Then an heiress married William Taliaferro, and when she died, her sister married the widower. Both of these families produced a number of distinguished citizens in Colonial days.

One of the Taliaferro couples had a beautiful daughter named Elizabeth. When she became a young lady, her father took her for a visit to London. There she met a handsome young English gentleman, with whom she fell deeply in love. They declared eternal faithfulness to each other and arranged to complete plans for their wedding by correspondence. Elizabeth's father, however, was adamantly against the match and intercepted the letters, so neither ever heard again from the other after Elizabeth had returned to Gloucester.

In time, as Elizabeth longed for her lost love, she fell ill and—apparently—died. Friends contended that she had lost the will to live and pined away. On a blustery November afternoon near sunset, they buried her in the family graveyard at the foot of the garden.

According to an account that has been handed down from generation to generation for more than a century, an irate butler, angered at some slight against him by the family, dug up Elizabeth's gravesite that night and opened the coffin to steal valuable jewelry that had been buried with her. One particular ring would not slip off her finger, so in his haste, the servant severed the finger.

To his horror, however, he found that the young woman was not dead! Though she had been presumed dead, she had merely lapsed into a deep cataleptic coma. The shock of having her finger cut off roused her, and she let out a moan. The terrified butler ran off into the night and was never heard from again. Somehow the frail Elizabeth, barefoot and thinly dressed, managed to climb out of the grave, crawl past the last dead stalks of the garden, and drag herself through a driving snowstorm—the first of the season—to the front porch of the house. There, in a weakened condition, she scratched feebly at the door.

If her father, sitting inside before a roaring fire, heard her, he likely dismissed it as one of the dogs trying to come in out of the storm and, lost in his grief, ignored the sound. The next morning, Elizabeth's body was found at the doorstep beneath a blanket of snow. She had frozen to death. A trail of blood led from the garden.

For years afterward, succeeding generations of Throckmortons and Taliaferros swore that manifestations of Elizabeth's ghost materialized in the house. Whenever the first snow of the year fell, they heard sounds of a rustling skirt ascending the staircase, followed by the distinct placing of logs in fireplaces and the crackle of a hearty fire in various rooms. Investigations would find no such logs or fires. Traces of blood would appear in the snow along the route Elizabeth had taken from the graveyard to the house. Such sights and sounds were attested to by various members of the families and their servants.

On one noteworthy occasion, generations later in 1879, Professor Warner Taliaferro, then head of the house, left one evening to spend the night at a friend's. Neighbors reported that in the midst of a fierce storm, they saw Church Hill ablaze with lights. Junius Browne Jr., passing by on horseback, rode up to the house to see if his sisters, visiting in the neighborhood, had sought shelter from the storm there. But no one was home. Servants living in quarters on the property also saw the lights and assumed Mr. Taliaferro had returned. He had not. This mystery was never solved.

The most compelling phenomenon, however, concerns the violets that grow in lush profusion near the steps to Church Hill. They are more beautiful and more plentiful here than in other parts of the grounds. It is said that they are watered by the tears of a dying young lady, seeking refuge from the season's first snow.

The Idiosyncrasies of "Mad Lucy"

Some called her, perhaps too generously, eccentric, capricious, whimsical, or odd. Others just said she was crazy. Regardless, it is certain that she was one of a kind, and her singular behavior caused excited titters of whispered gossip in the upper strata of eighteenth-century social circles on two continents. Had she not been from a well-to-do family, she probably would have been committed to a mental institution early in her life. As it was, her actions were covered up, embarrassedly laughed off, or explained away as being those of a high-strung young lady with a flair for mischief.

Her name was Lucy Ludwell. She married John Paradise, a scholar and linguist, and an accepted member of the intellectual set in England, which in those days surrounded the eminent Dr. Samuel Johnson. Lucy lived much of her life in London and, according to one published account, "startled city society by such exploits as dashing boiling water from her tea urn on a too-garrulous gentleman who annoyed her."

Early in the eighteenth century, her grandfather built a town residence in Williamsburg, a handsome brick mansion surrounded by stables, a paddock, smokehouse, "necessary" house, and wood-house near the kitchen. A garden featured a prized dwarf boxwood collection. Property Lucy inherited in Virginia was confiscated by the commonwealth during the Revolutionary War, because the politics espoused by her husband were counter to the cause of the colonists fighting for their freedom. In 1805, however, ten years after her husband died, Lucy set sail for America and was allowed to take up residence in what has become known as Ludwell-Paradise House on historic Duke of Gloucester Street in Williamsburg.

It was here, as she grew older, that she again became the talk of the town with her peculiar habits. For openers, Lucy, because of her social position in London, considered herself above her friends and neighbors in Virginia. She had a haughty attitude that she made no effort to disguise. It is said that she held court at her house and didn't object in the least to being called Madam.

Another of Lucy's quirks was her penchant for borrowing the new clothes of her lady friends, especially hats. She viewed herself as a fashion plate of the times and seemed oblivious to the fact that everyone in town knew when she was garbed in loaned clothing. On Sundays, the congregation of her church always got a chuckle, because Lucy regularly had her "little black boy," a servant's son, carry her prayer book into church ahead of her, as if to announce her imminent entrance.

"Mad Lucy" is probably best remembered for entertaining guests on weird carriage rides—weird in that they never went anywhere. She had a favorite coach reassembled on the back porch of her house. When callers dropped by, she invited them into the coach, and then had it rolled back and forth across the porch on imaginary trips by a servant.

Her fantasy carriage rides became so frequent, and her other peculiarities so pronounced, that Lucy began having difficulty differentiating between the worlds of make-believe and reality. Eventually, in 1812, she was committed to the state asylum

Lucy died two years later, but her spirit apparently remains entrenched in the Ludwell-Paradise House, a favorite stop on the nightly Williamsburg ghost tours. A number of house occupants over the years have reported hearing strange sounds not attributable to any natural source. Most notable of the witnesses are Rudolph Bares and his wife. Bares is a retired vice president of the Colonial

Williamsburg Foundation who lived in the house for several years in the 1960s and 1970s.

"Oh, we never heard any ghostly voices, saw any levitations, or anything like that," he says. "But my wife and I each experienced the same odd phenomenon on numerous different occasions. And that is, we would be downstairs when we would hear the water running in a second-floor bathtub. Then we would hear a splashing sound in the tub, as if someone were taking a bath. The first few times we heard it, we went up the stairs to take a look, but there was never anything or anyone there, and no water was in the tub. It was bone dry. So after a while, we wouldn't even check when we heard it. We'd just laugh and say it must be Lucy pouring a bath for herself."

Cleanliness, it should be noted, was another of Mad Lucy's idiosyncrasies. She was known to have taken as many as six to eight baths a day.

Hooded Visions Rise from the Mist

One of the most knowledgeable experts on Colonial Williamsburg history is the now-retired Reverend Dick Carter, who tells of a humorous incident that occurred about forty years ago. It was the middle of winter, when tourism was way down, and five Colonial Williamsburg historical interpreters were invited to tour and learn the history of St. Peters Episcopal Church in neighboring New Kent County. Because of the misty weather, the ladies, in addition to their Colonial costumes, were all wearing long cloaks with hoods.

As they left the church after their tour, it was just past sunset, and the ladies sat on a bench in front of the church cemetery to await their ride back to Williamsburg. Pretty soon they heard a vehicle coming up the driveway and assumed it was for them. "Now picture this in your mind's eye," Reverend Carter says. "These five women, in their Colonial costumes with long cloaks and hoods over their heads, arose in unison . . . in the dusk . . . in the mist . . . and with the tombstones in the background. And it wasn't their ride. It was a tourist from New Jersey who was lost!

"The ladies said the man let out an audible gasp, slammed his foot down on the accelerator, and promptly drove into a tree! He then backed up and sped off, spinning his tires, without even bothering to stop and see what damage he had done to the car."

The Curse Tree of Jamestown Island

In 2007, Jamestown, the location of the first English colony in America, celebrated its four hundredth anniversary, an event attended by the Queen of England and many other dignitaries. Not covered in the media blitz that recorded the occasion was a little-known legend of possible paranormal activity at the site.

Just beyond Jamestown Memorial Church, which was built in 1907 on the foundation of the original church erected in 1617, lies a small, quiet, tree-shaded cemetery containing only a handful of graves. It is here that James and Sarah Harrison Blair are buried.

Blair was an important figure in the commonwealth's history during the latter days of the seventeenth century and well into the eighteenth. He served as councilor to the British governor and has been described by biographers as a very powerful man and the chief force behind the founding of the College of William and Mary, the second-oldest institution of higher learning in the country. On a more personal note, his tombstone points out that "the comliness [sic] of a handsome face adorned him . . . he entertained elegantly in a cheerful, hospitable manner without luxury . . . in affability, he excelled."

In 1687, Sarah Harrison, then a strikingly beautiful young lady of seventeen, was an active participant in the plantation circle social life along the lower James River. The oldest daughter of the "mighty" Colonel Benjamin Harrison of Wakefield Plantation, a wealthy landowner, she was vivacious, full of life, and headstrong. Despite this strongly independent nature, or perhaps because of it, in conjunction with her natural beauty, Sarah was actively wooed by a number of handsome and eligible suitors.

Thus it was that, in 1687, according to Sam Robinson, a longtime caretaker at Jamestown Island, "she firs' sign a marriage contract with a young gentleman by name of William Roscoe. He was twenty-two and she was seventeen." The contract, Robinson says, stated that "she would never marry to any man on earth other than Roscoe as long as she was alive, so hep her God, signed Sarah Harrison."

Three weeks later, however, she met the charismatic Blair and was swept off her feet. Her parents were not so enchanted. There were two immediate problems. First, she already was engaged to a perfectly acceptable young man. And second, James Blair at the time was thirty-one years old, nearly twice Sarah's age. What immediately ensued was the expected: a bitter rift between daughter and parents. This intensified when Sarah broke her initial engagement and told them she planned to marry Blair. Through reasoning, arguments, and threats, her parents tried everything to discourage the union, but Sarah's mind was made up.

James and Sarah were promptly married, although it is not known whether her parents attended the affair. They would not give up even after the wedding and sought to have the marriage annulled. But here fate took a curious turn. In Robinson's words: "Colonel Benjamin, Mrs. Hannah, his wife, and his baby daughter—all three of them was killed up on Route 5 at Berkeley Plantation by lightning, so they didn't get a chance in life to separate Miss Sarah from Dr. Blair."

The couple, it is said, lived a happy life together as husband and wife. She died in 1713 at the age of forty-two, still not forgiven by her family. "For disobeying her parents in life," says Robinson, "the Harrisons buried her some feet away from the family." Her husband lived on for thirty more years, contributing significantly to the continued growth and prosperity of the young colony. When he died in 1743, he was laid to rest at a site six inches to the left of his wife's grave.

In 1750, seven years after Blair's death, fate intervened again. Robinson tells what happened: "Was a stoned-in fence around the two graves six inches apart, side by side. A sycamore tree came up between 'em as a little wild sapling. Wasn't anythin' deed to prevent de tree or protect de graves, so as it growed, it caught in the center tomb there by Dr. Blair, break the stones then in two, both ends, right where her stone were joined to Dr. Blair stone, push her tomb up out de grown' above Dr. Blair, and push de back on the head end seven feet from her husband back over to de right, within six inches of her sister, mother, father, and another sister . . . and leave Dr. Blair on de left hand side in a stone by himself."

And so the legend arose: Sarah's parents, who could not dissolve her marriage with Blair while they were alive, finally were able to separate the lovers after death. The late Robert Ripley wrote about this odd incident in his "Believe It or Not" column, calling the sycamore the "mother-in-law" tree. Others have referred to it as the "curse tree." Robinson, who told the story many times, once to

Queen Elizabeth of England during her visit to Jamestown in 1957 on the 350th anniversary of the first settlers' landing, says, "The mother-in-law didn't get a chance in life to separate her daughter, Sarah, from Dr. Blair, but she did come back and plant the old sycamore to separate her."

There is a bizarre footnote to the story. Several years ago, the old sycamore tree, which had grown to gigantic size, died and was cut out of the site, although the broken bricks and cracked tombs were left as they were, pushed apart. Soon after, a new sycamore sapling sprang up in the exact same spot where the original tree had stood. It flourishes today. It is due, some believe, to Sarah's parents reasserting their will from beyond the grave.

Aunt Pratt's Portrait

Shirley Plantation is unquestionably one of the most magnificent original Colonial mansions in the United States. Architectural historians believe that parts of its impressive design were inspired by the governor's palace in Williamsburg. The site on which the great house sits is steeped in early Virginia history and tradition. It was, in fact, founded in 1613, just six years after the first settlers landed at Jamestown and a full seven years before the Pilgrims arrived at Plymouth Rock.

Shirley Plantation is located at a point overlooking a scenic bend in the James River, about halfway between Williamsburg and Richmond. The estate has been in the Hill and Carter families for more than three hundred years. The present house was begun in 1723 by the third Edward Hill, a man of status in the colony. He built it for his daughter Elizabeth, who married John Carter, son of the legendary wealthy planter Robert "King" Carter. It took nearly fifty years to complete the construction, which was done, as one author describes it, "with a lavish disregard for cost seldom displayed in the building of even great mansions."

The handsome brick house stands three stories tall, with rows of dormer windows projecting from the roof on all sides. It has twin chimneys flanking a large carved pineapple, the Colonial symbol for hospitality. Two splendid two-story porticoes, each with four white pillars, set off the front of the building with stylish grace. Inside, eighteenth-century artisans fashioned superb paneling and delicate carvings. A major design feature is an elegant carved walnut staircase that rises for three stories without visible support—the only one of its kind in America. The entire house is filled with exquisite furnishings, crested silver, and interesting memorabilia assembled from the ten generations of the families that have lived here.

Shirley was a well-known center of hospitality a hundred years before and during the American Revolution. George Washington and Thomas Jefferson were guests here, as were numerous other prominent Virginians. There are many interesting anecdotes and stories about events that have transpired at Shirley. One of the more charming concerns the time a young and beautiful Anne Hill Carter was carrying a punchbowl across the dining room when it began slipping from her fingers. She was rescued by a dashing young military officer, "Light Horse" Harry Lee. Not long afterward, they were married at Shirley. Their son became one of the most famous of all Virginians: Robert E. Lee.

Perhaps the most intriguing legend revolves around the ghost of a former resident and family member, for Shirley, like a number of its neighboring plantations along the James River, is allegedly haunted. Aunt Pratt was reportedly a sister of Edward Hill. Little is known of the woman, who was born late in the seventeenth century, but it is said there always was a certain air of mystery about her.

One of the things Shirley is noted for is its fine collection of family portraits. Aunt Pratt's painting occupied a desirable place in an upstairs bedroom for a number of years after her death. Then, as a new generation of the family took over occupancy and decided to redecorate, the portrait was taken down and banished to the obscurity of the attic.

Apparently Aunt Pratt's spirit did not take kindly to this. In fact, she made what family members described as a "mighty disturbance." This usually took the form of the sound of a woman rocking in the attic late at night. In addition to the Hills and Carters, a number of guests told of hearing the incessant rocking. Yet when anyone summoned courage to check the attic, all was still and quiet. Eventually the restlessness of her spirit proved too much for the occupants of the house, and they prudently chose to bring the portrait back down and hang it in its proper place. Once this was done, the strange sounds were never heard again.

It seems, however, that this did not end the troubles caused by Aunt Pratt. In the early 1970s, the Virginia Travel Council scoured about the commonwealth in search of relics, antiques, and other items associated with psychic phenomena for a tourist promotion exhibition they were hosting in New York City. Council officials, having heard the story of Aunt Pratt's ghostly rocking, asked if they might borrow the portrait for the exhibit, so it was crated and shipped north. But no sooner had the portrait been hung on a wall than Aunt Pratt apparently once again came to life, openly venting her displeasure at being so far away from home.

According to credible witnesses, the portrait was observed swinging in its display case. People walking by on the street said it was constantly moving and swayed back and forth so violently that other exhibits were also vibrating. A network news program reported on the phenomenon. Then one morning, workmen found the portrait lying on the floor several feet away from its case and, in their words, "heading toward the exit."

As a security measure, officials had Aunt Pratt's portrait locked up in a closet when not on exhibit. One night, a maintenance crew became unnerved when they heard knocking and crying coming from the locked room. No living mortal was inside. The next morning, the portrait had mysteriously "escaped" from the closet and was lying on the floor outside.

At this point, a psychic expert was called in. She studied the portrait carefully and felt strong sensations. The psychic believed that two women were involved in the portrait and offered two theories in possible explanation. One was that there were actually two portraits, one painted on top of the other. The supposition was that the original lady involved had, perhaps for centuries, been struggling to regain her identity and respect. The other was that a model perhaps sat in for Aunt Pratt during the painting, again pointing to the conceivability of a deep-rooted identity crisis.

Whether or not either of these ideas had any validity, the psychic expert was convinced that a powerful spiritual phenomenon was indeed associated with the portrait; that the person involved was somehow trying to convey her irritation at being, to her mind, indignantly displayed. Some parapsychology experts maintain that spirits that manifest in the manner Aunt Pratt did are actually ghosts of residents who believe, even though they are long dead and gone, that the houses they lived in still belong to them. This seems the most plausible explanation in Aunt Pratt's case.

Subsequent events added credence to this line of thought. On its way back south from the New York showing, the portrait was taken to a shop in Richmond so repairs could be made on the now-battered frame. When it was picked up, the shop owner said that ever since Aunt Pratt had been in his care, he heard bells ringing. He deemed this odd, because there were no bells in his shop.

When the portrait finally reached Shirley and was properly hung in its accustomed place, the manifestations ceased, and Aunt Pratt has not been heard from again—with one notable exception. Right beneath the painting is a large mahogany chest. One afternoon a few years ago, a historical interpreter at Shirley was telling the story of Aunt Pratt's adventures to a group of tourists. When she finished, one man, standing directly beneath the portrait, said that was the biggest bunch of baloney he had ever heard.

As he said it, the doors of the chest suddenly sprang open and banged him sharply on his backside. The room emptied in ten seconds flat!

Comfort from Beyond

In the home of Janice and Eldridge Busic Jr. in Honaker, Russell County, hangs a portrait of a beautiful young woman. No one seems to know who she is or where the picture came from. When Eldridge's parents bought the house in the 1940s, the portrait was already there.

In 1998, the Busics were showing their home to some friends. One of them, James Boyd, describes what happened: "As we entered a room on the upper floor, I noticed an old picture of a young woman in Victorian dress hanging on the wall. I walked over and ran my hand over the frame. At that moment, I felt a chill run over me, and every hair on my body stood on end. As I turned away, I was told that there was an interesting tale about the picture. I said, 'There has to be. Look at the goose bumps on my arm!'"

The legend behind the portrait is this: about forty years ago, a young woman from New York came to town to teach at the local elementary school and boarded with the Busics. She left after a few years but returned in 1983 to visit the couple. She asked Janice if she could go upstairs and see the portrait. When she came back downstairs, she was pale and silent. Then she described something that happened on her first night in the house. "When I went to bed, the moon was shining through the window, and I couldn't go to sleep. Everything seemed strange and odd.

"And then a beautiful woman with long hair came into the room. She came over and crawled into bed with me. For some reason, I wasn't frightened at all. I turned slightly until my head rested on her soft, long hair, and I went to sleep feeling safe and secure. When I awakened the next morning, the woman was gone. Instead of going downstairs to the bathroom I had been assigned, I decided to look for a bathroom upstairs. As I passed through a bedroom, there on the wall, before my very eyes, was the portrait of the same lovely young woman with whom I had slept!"

Shortly before her 1983 visit, the woman had lost her younger brother, who was killed in an auto accident. "I could not accept his death, and I was losing faith and all the beliefs that had been dear to me. Then one night, the same beautiful young lady with the long, soft hair, wearing a flowing chiffon gown, came into my room where I was then living. With the sweetest smile I have ever seen, she said my brother had sent her back to comfort me. 'He wants you to know that he has never been as happy before, nor known such joy.' She told me secrets that only my brother and I shared. Nobody else could possibly know the things she told me. Then she said that he wants you to promise never to worry about him again. When she left the room, a great warmth and sense of peace engulfed me. I slept soundly for the first time since my brother's death.

"And yes," she told the Busics, "she was the same woman as the one in the portrait in your bedroom!"

A few years later, as Janice Busic was walking through her bedroom, she stopped and, on impulse, placed her hand on the portrait. The curved glass covering the picture, which had been maintained with loving care for decades, cracked!

The Transforming Portrait

In 1965, Cary and Gibson McConnaughey bought historic Haw Branch Plantation in Amelia County, about thirty miles southwest of Richmond. "I was nine years old," Gibson says, "when my grandmother first brought me out to see Haw Branch, because the home had been in our family from the time the plantation was established in 1745 until after the Civil War." Cary and Gibson have carefully and lovingly restored the house and grounds.

The past half century has seen many manifestations of psychic phenomena at Haw Branch. The most intriguing involves a portrait, a large pastel rendering of a young woman named Florence Wright. She was a distant relative by marriage, and little was known of her except that she died before the painting was completed, although she was only in her twenties.

After two decades in storage, the portrait was given to the McConnaugheys by a cousin, who told them it was a colored painting with beautiful pastels. This initially bewildered Gibson, who says that "when the picture was uncrated and the massive gilt rococo frame and glass were painstakingly dusted, the portrait appeared to be a charcoal rendering. No color was evident; everything was either a dirty white, gray, or black." No signature of the artist was to be found, and the back of the frame was tightly sealed. It was left that way and hung over the library fireplace.

One day a few months later, Cary was sitting in the library reading a newspaper, when he looked up and noticed that the rose in the portrait seemed to have taken on a pink tinge. The girl's black hair also was beginning to lighten, and her grayish skin was turning flesh-colored. These changes continued gradually over the next year, until the portrait miraculously transformed into pastel brilliance.

Says Gibson: "A partially opened rose in the portrait began to take on a definite pink cast, when previously it had been grayish white. Other changes continued for over a year. Several experts connected with art departments at Virginia colleges saw the picture from the time of its arrival and confirmed the change in coloring but could offer no logical explanation."

A psychic who came to investigate said that Florence Wright's spirit was tied to the portrait because she died before it was finished, and that she had the power to remove the color from it when she was dissatisfied with where it was placed. She apparently liked Haw Branch, and therefore restored the original color.

"Who can say his theory isn't correct?" asks Gibson. "Today the girl's clear blue eyes look rather sadly out beneath her curly reddish brown hair, and her pink and white complexion looks as if she were alive. The green and beige upholstery on the gnome-carved gilt chair she sits in is a deeper shade of the carved jade jar on a table next to her. The rose that was first seen to change color slightly is now a clear, soft pink."

In 1971, Gibson wrote: "Much about the portrait still remains a mystery. How did the young girl die? Did the partially opened pink rosebud in the crystal vase foretell her early death, or was it added symbolically after she died? Who was the artist, and why did the pastel portrait's coloring change without human assistance? There may be a slight lead on the artist's name. When the portrait first arrived, I was told that it was painted by a famous American artist and signed by him, but no one remembered his name."

About a year later, some of her questions were answered—in a most curious fashion. One summer evening in 1972, one of Gibson's daughters and a friend of hers were sitting on the floor in the library beneath the portrait. They moved over to the sofa, and seconds later the supports of the picture's heavy frame pulled loose. The painting slowly slid down the wall until the bottom of the frame reached the mantel shelf, where it crushed a row of porcelain antiques, tipped slightly forward, and fell to the wide pine floorboards. As the girls sat transfixed, glass shattered all across the floor. The portrait had fallen facedown on the exact spot where they had been sitting only moments before.

"Although the painting itself was not damaged, the big wooden frame was broken," says Gibson. "Lifting it up, we found, underneath what had been the tightly sealed backing, a brass plate that gave the girl's full name, her birth date, and the date of her death. Though we searched for the artist's signature, it could not be found. The next day, the frame was repaired, the portrait placed back in it, and the glass replaced. The man who did the work searched as carefully as we did to find the artist's name, but without success.

"It was late in the day when we arrived back at Haw Branch with the portrait. The sun was red and low in the sky. As Cary and I lifted the picture from the back of the station wagon, I happened to tilt my end of the frame slightly upward. Suddenly, as though a red neon sign had been lit, the name of 'J. Wells Champney' appeared. It had been signed in pencil on the apron of the dark mahogany table in the picture. Only under a certain angle of light could it be seen."

The McConnaugheys later learned that the girl in the portrait had been born into a wealthy family. Her parents commissioned Champney to paint the portrait. Before it could be completed, however, Florence Wright, at the age of twenty-four, slumped over a piano keyboard and died of a massive stroke. The artist then added a partially opened rose to signify that his subject had died an untimely death before the painting could be completed. It was also discovered that Champney was killed soon after, when he fell down an elevator shaft in New York City.

"Many say that they can see the girl blush when they stare hard at the portrait," says Gibson. "But now that Florence's portrait has regained its original luster and hangs in a permanent home she apparently likes, it seems unlikely that she will ever again change the color."

The Phantom Friend of the Oystermen

At Fort Eustis, an active U.S. Army base halfway between Newport News and Williamsburg, there is a small, sheltered cove where the waters of Nell's Creek feed into the James River. Decades ago, before the government purchased the land surrounding this area, Nell's Creek was a haven for local oystermen. Daily they would ply their time-honored trade amid the rich oyster beds of the river nearby, and some would stay in the mouth of the creek from Monday night until Friday, when they would take their catch to market and head home.

A local legend has it that this creek was named for a young lady called Nell who lived in the region in the late nineteenth century. No one seems to know her last name. It is said that she was a spirited, headstrong young woman who fell in love with a man described as a straggler, and her father strongly objected to such a union. He told her that if she violated his wishes and married the man, he would kill her and bury her, along with all his money.

Despite the dire warning, she ran off with her lover, and her father lived up to his threat. He killed her and buried her, supposedly along with his life's savings, at a point on or near the creek, beneath two large walnut trees. Since that time, from the 1880s up to the 1930s, Nell was said to frequently reappear, mostly through the psychic manifestation of knockings or rappings, to area oystermen. She was apparently a friendly ghost, who provided timely news on where the best oystering was from day to day, and she often played games in which she seemed to enjoy answering questions, mostly concerning numbers and figures. Why she chose to befriend the lonely watermen is a question that remains unanswered.

The legend is best told by an elderly retired oysterman known as J. P. In the 1920s and 1930s, he worked the James regularly with his father and a brother. "I definitely believe she was there," he says. "There's no doubt in my mind. I'm not a superstitious person, or necessarily a believer in ghosts, but in this instance I do believe. I only experienced her presence once, but it was something I will never forget. My father and brother heard her many times, and they believed. Some say it was all a myth, but a lot of people heard her."

J. P. says the stories about Nell began in the late nineteenth century. No one ever saw her; they heard her. She "appeared" by knocking on the cabin roofs of the oystermen's boats. "It was a knock unlike any other I have ever heard," J. P. recalls. "It was different. I can't even describe it. I guess I was about eighteen or twenty when I experienced it. We were laid up overnight in the cove, and I was standing outside the cabin with my head tucked inside, listening to the conversation. There was a very distinct knocking on top of the cabin. When I poked my head outside, it sounded like it came from inside. And when I ducked my head inside the cabin, it sounded like it came from the outside. There was no way it could have been a hoax. I wasn't really scared, but I must have looked concerned, because someone laughed and said, 'That's just old Nell.'"

J. P.'s father told him many times about the rappings, saying that Nell "talked" through her knockings. One rap meant yes, and two no. "In those days, people oystered over many sites up and down the river," J. P. continues. "Some would come out of the Warwick River, Deep Creek, Squashers Hole, and other places. Every rock in the river had a name, and the oystermen knew them all. So they would ask Nell how their peers were doing at other locations. Like, they would ask her how many bushels of oysters they got today at Thomas' Rock, near the James River Bridge, and Nell would give so many knocks."

If the harvests were better elsewhere, according to J. P., then those asking the questions of Nell would fish those waters the next day. Invariably, their hauls improved. "Only a few took stock in all this," J. P. says, "but those who did always benefited from the spectral advice. And she was always right. If she said so many bushels were brought in at such and such a rock, it was so."

Nell amazed the men with all sorts of revelations. "She could answer anything she was asked," J. P. says. "You could ask her how many children someone had, and she would rap out the number in knocks on the cabin. You could ask her someone's age, and she knew it exactly. My father said one time a man grabbed a handful of beans out of a sack and asked her how many he had. She told him—to the bean!"

In this manner, Nell carried on conversations with a number of oystermen over the years. She was especially conversant with one man, J. P. says. "I was told that when he died, she even appeared at his funeral by rapping on his coffin!"

Robert Forest recalls his ancestors talking about Nell. "I've heard the stories," he says. "The one I remember best concerned an old man named John, who was a very religious fellow. He had heard about Nell too, and he didn't believe the stories until the night he experienced the sensation himself. He went out with some oystermen once just to prove there was nothing to the tale. He carried his Bible with him. Well, they laid up in Deep Creek that night and tried to raise her. 'Nell,' they said, 'if you're here, rap twice on the cabin.' Nothing happened. About thirty minutes later, they tried again, and sure enough, this time there were two sharp raps. John still wasn't convinced. He thought someone was playing a trick on him, so he went out on deck. There was no one there, and no boats nearby. John became a believer right then."

Occasionally Nell became disturbed at something asked or said, and she would quickly make her displeasure known. Another waterman said he heard oystermen tell of the time she rocked their boat so violently they thought the tong shafts in the cabin would break. Yet outside, the waters of the creek were "as smooth as a dish."

J. P. says his brother was reading out of the Bible to her one night from the chapter of Deuteronomy, when the knockings on the cabin became louder and louder and "got out of control." He stopped reading and she stopped. Deuteronomy, it may be remembered, includes the Ten Commandments, among which are "Thou shalt not kill" and "Honor thy father and mother." No wonder Nell was upset.

"All she ever told us was that her father had killed her and buried her nearby with his money," J. P. says. "So one time my father and brother went off digging in an area where there were two large walnut trees. The whole time they were there, however, they were pestered by large hornets and wasps, and they had to give it up." Others also went looking for the lost treasure. Once they were driven off by a swarm of bees. Another time a sudden storm whipped up, and the wind nearly took down one of the trees. That scared them off, and they never came back.

"I sure wish I could talk to old Nell again," J. P. says. "I've tried many times, but she's never answered." In fact, no one has heard from Nell for several decades. She was a friend of the oystermen for half a century or so, but when the military took over at Fort Eustis, the knockings ceased.

"She must be at peace now," J. P. surmises.

The Spirited Revenge of Dolly Mammy

Poquoson is located on a patch of land between Seaford and Yorktown to the north and west, and just above Hampton to the south and east. It derives its colorful name from the Algonquin Indian word *pocosin*, which means a swamp or dismal place. It is nearly surrounded by water and is adjacent to the Plum Tree Island National Wildlife Refuge. Since Colonial times, Poquoson has been the home of rugged and closely knit clans of watermen and farmers. Many current families can date their ancestors in the area back hundreds of years.

For eons, residents owning cattle let their animals roam freely in lush, marshy regions known locally as "the Commons." Such was the case with a woman known as "Dolly Mammy" Messick, whose tragic story and haunting reappearances have been remembered and recounted from generation to generation.

On a cold, blustery day in November 1904, with heavy dark clouds hovering over the lowlands and the forecast of a snowstorm, Dolly asked her two teenage daughters, Minnie and Lettie Jane, to go with her to bring in the family cow. Ensconced comfortably before a fire in the farmhouse, the girls refused to budge. Angrily flinging on a cloak, Dolly turned to them and said that if anything happened to her, she would return to haunt them for the rest of their lives. The girls just shrugged. With that, the mother disappeared into the gloom.

When she had not come back by dark, a search party of friends and neighbors was hastily organized, and they tramped through the marshes with lanterns, calling her name, but they found nothing. The next morning, a lone fisherman, easing his boat up Bell's Oyster Gut, a narrow estuary near the woman's home, was startled at the sight of a bare human leg sticking up out of the marsh grasses. He went for help, and soon after, the body of Dolly Mammy was recovered. She apparently had been sucked into a pocket of quicksand. It appeared that she had struggled desperately for her life, because the rushes and grasses around her body had been pulled up. Her funeral was well attended.

Not long after that, her haunting threat began to be carried out. One day, the girls went to visit nearby relatives. No sooner had they arrived than ghostly knockings began to echo loudly throughout the house. Suspecting pranksters, a family member grabbed a heavy piece of wood and barred the door. Incredibly, the bar leaped into the air from its iron fastenings and flew across the room. The knockings, which sounded like a fist of iron against a thin board, continued and grew in intensity, so much so that they were heard a quarter of a mile away by the master of the house. Rushing back home, he found the girls and his family cowering in terror.

While the thunderous knockings that seemed to follow the girls wherever they went, especially at their house, continued as the main form of spectral manifestation, many other phenomena occurred as well. "All sorts of things started to happen," says Randolph Rollins, a spry octogenarian and lifelong resident of Poquoson. Rollins's grandfather was a witness to some of the paranormal events.

"One night, the two girls slept together in a bed, and the next morning when they woke up, their hair was tightly braided together," Rollins says. "No one could ever explain that." As the months passed, relatives and neighbors spent considerable time at Dolly's house trying to console the distraught daughters. Rollins's grandfather was one of them.

"He told me many a time about being in the house when a table in the middle of the living room with a lamp on it would start shaking and jumping up and down. Then the lamp would go out and it would be dark, and he could hear the sounds of someone being slapped. When he relit the lamp, the girls would have red marks on their faces with the imprint of a hand. That happened a number of times."

One witness claimed that as the girls lay in deep sleep in the bed one night, something lifted the bed off the floor and shook it. Another time, an unseen hand snatched a Bible from beneath the pillow of one of the girls and flung it against the wall.

As word of the strange incidents got around, curiosity seekers from all over came to the house. A U.S. Army officer from nearby Fort Monroe arrived with the intention of debunking the ghost as a myth. He had his men search the house from cellar to attic, and then had guards surround it to ward off any tricksters. Yet that evening, as he sat in the parlor, the knockings were so loud they could be heard half a mile away. Then a lamp seemed to lift itself from a table, sailed through the room, and landed on the mantel. Having seen and heard enough, the bewildered officer wrote in a report, "Whatever causes the disturbances is of supernatural origin."

Rollins adds that once when his grandfather was in the house, two skeptical lawyers showed up. The rappings grew so deafening that normal conversation couldn't be heard, and they abruptly left. One memorable evening, a spirit medium was invited to hold a séance in the home. It was attended by the girls and a large group of people. According to published accounts of the affair, a shadowy figure appeared, winding a ball of yarn. As the figure responded to various commands of the medium, the girls fainted. Then the medium said, "If you are the mother of these girls and are connected with these curious rappings," which were going on simultaneously, "speak!" The girls' names were then called out, followed by wild, shrieking laughter. That was enough to clear the room.

This single appearance seemed to be the high point of the hauntings. When one of the girls died some time later, the knockings and other phenomena ceased. Dolly Mammy had made good her threat.

Today, in the lush marshes and thick grass of the Commons, through which the Poquoson cows roamed freely, there is one small patch of land where, oddly, no vegetation has grown since the early twentieth century. It is precisely the spot where the body of Dolly Mammy was found so long ago.

Three Pink Rose Petals

A few years ago, a woman approached me as I was signing books at the annual Newport News Fall Festival, held the first weekend each October. Shyly, she said that she had something to tell me, but I wouldn't believe her. I told her that in my business of writing about ghosts, I hear that a lot. This is her story. She wishes to remain anonymous, so for the sake of clarity, let's call her Jane.

When Jane was twelve years old, growing up in the Tidewater area, her grandmother died and was buried in a pearl gray suit. As some men were lowering the casket into the ground, Jane walked over and dropped three pink rose petals on top of the casket, because her grandmother had always loved pink roses.

Thirty-some years later, Jane, now an adult, was in the hospital for a serious cancer operation. It was touch and go. It wasn't known whether she was going to live or die, and the operation was the last hope. Her family was very concerned. She was confined to the intensive care ward, allowed no visitors, no flowers—nothing.

Just before the orderlies came in to take her to the operating room, a vision of her long-dead grandmother suddenly appeared to her. Her grandmother was wearing the same pearl gray suit she had been buried in more than three decades earlier. The vision spoke, saying in a comforting manner, "Don't worry, you will live to see your children's children!" With that, the apparitional figure dematerialized.

The orderlies then came in. As they lifted Jane from her hospital bed to a gurney, three pink rose petals fluttered to the floor.

The Ordeal by Touch

Superstition was strong in Colonial Virginia, even before the infamous witch trials occurred in Salem, Massachusetts, in the 1690s, and in the well-documented case of Grace Sherwood, a suspected witch in the Old Dominion. Such superstition was brought over to the New World with the settlers, ancient beliefs in the bizarre handed down family to family for centuries in Europe.

One of the weirdest of these old rituals was known as the "ordeal by touch." For some unexplained reason, it was thought by some that if a murderer touched or came into the presence of the body of his or her victim, the wounds that had been inflicted on the deceased would bleed afresh. This archaic custom can be traced to seventeenth-century England and Scotland, where it was widely prevalent even among educated people.

Michael Drayton, an English poet of that era, penned:

> If the vile actors of the heinous deed
> Near the dead body happily be brought,
> Oft has been prov'd the breathless corpse will bleed.

Even William Shakespeare was drawn into the tradition. He wrote the following in Act I, Scene II, of *Richard III*, where Lady Anne, in the presence of the body of the dead king, is made to accuse Gloster in this passage:

> O gentlemen, see, see, dead Henry's wounds
> Open their congeal'd mouths and bleed afresh!
> Blush, blush, thou lump of foul deformity,
> For 'tis thy presence that exhales this blood
> From cold and empty veins, where no blood dwells?

There are at least two recorded instances of actual cases where the ordeal by touch occurred in Virginia, documented in court records. One in the records of Northampton County, which state, "On December 14, 1656, Captain William Whittington issued a warrant for a Jury of Inquest over the body of Paul Rynners," suspected to have been murdered by William Custis. The jury reported: "We have viewed the body of Paul Rynners, late of this county and deceased & and have caused Wm. Custis to touch the face and stroke the body of said victim which he willingly did. But no sign did appear unto us of question in the law." Custis was thus freed.

The second incident involved the alleged murder of an infant, born of Mary Andrews of Accomack, on the Eastern Shore of Virginia. Mary was the unmarried daughter of Sarah Carter and the stepdaughter of Paul Carter. Both Paul and Sarah were accused of the crime and brought to trial. The following is from Accomack court records:

Att a Court held and continued for Accomack County, March 18, 1679. Question. What doe yu know concerning a child born of Mary the daughter of Sarah, the wife of the said Paul? Answere. That he doth know that the said Mary had a man child born of her body and that the said Sarah assisted at the birth of the said child, & that he certainly knoweth not whether it were born alive or not & that they did endeavor to preserve the life thereof and that it lay betwixt his wife and her daughter all night and that ye next morning he saw it dead & he and his wife carefully buried the said child but that his wife carefully washing and dressed it.

The body of the baby was exhumed so that it could be "stroaked" by the accused couple. A jury consisting of twelve women was assembled. Paul Carter was found guilty of the crime, because while he was "stroaking" the child, "black and sotted places" on its body grew "fresh and red."

It is not specified what punishment Paul was given. This, however, is said to have been the last instance of trial by the ordeal by touch on record.

An Obsession Named Melanie

Mary Bowman is a vivacious, red-haired, admitted workaholic who ran a successful interior design business in Virginia Beach. She also is, as she describes it, metaphysical. "To me," she says, "that simply means open. You go beyond the five senses which are earthbound." The layperson would probably call Mary psychic. She has had a special sensitivity since childhood. When she was ten, for instance, she had a vivid dream in which her grandfather died. She awoke and told her parents. They told her to go back to sleep. An hour later, the telephone rang, and the family was informed of the grandfather's death.

"Oh, yes, I've had some weird experiences over the years," Mary says with a smile. But nothing prepared her for what happened in the fall of 1985. After working late in her office one night, she got in her car and headed home. As she was driving past an old farm on Greatneck Road, she felt a sensation. "There was a voice," she remembers. "It was a girl's voice, and it was crying out for help." It was not unusual for Mary to receive such a message. She often "reads" the troubled thoughts of others in daily contacts with people and has had to learn how to turn off such waves. But this girl's voice was different. It sounded urgent, and it seemed as if she had singled out Mary for a specific purpose.

As time went on, the sensation grew stronger. Each time Mary drove past that section of the city, she would hear the voice calling out. She began to form a mental image. "It scared me at first," she says, "because she looked so much like my daughter. I saw a picture of a young girl, maybe eighteen or nineteen. She had long, blond hair. She was lying down, as if she were in a coffin. She appeared to be wearing Colonial-era clothes, with billowing sleeves. I got the feeling that she lived two hundred years ago."

Mary saw other distinct features as well. She envisioned a big, meandering farmhouse with a large porch in white latticework, part of which was broken. And very sharp in the image was a brick wall. Mary felt that all these things were connected. "I became obsessed with it. I took off from my work in the middle of the day and would drive around looking for the house and brick wall. Things got crazy. I had to find out about the girl. Who was she? What did she want? Why was she calling to me? I became a nervous wreck!"

Mary went to a friend who was also psychic. "She immediately identified with me," Mary says. "She saw the same thing I did. We felt that the name of the girl was Melanie, and she might have been a schoolteacher. She had an affair with a married man and had gotten pregnant. We sensed that her lover had killed her and hastily buried her in an unmarked grave."

It was at this point that Mary says she had to let go. "I wanted to help, but it had become so overpowering I was afraid the search for Melanie would consume me." For the next several months, Mary went about her life, blocking out the vision.

Then one day, as she was in the area of the old farm, she saw it—the brick wall, just as she had visualized. It surrounded the farmhouse, separating it from the rows of new houses that were being developed all around. Instinctively, Mary went up to the door of the house and knocked. When the owner answered, she told him the story of her obsessive dream from start to finish, including the brick wall.

"I was afraid he would think I had escaped from the mental ward," she says, "but he hardly seemed surprised. In fact, he just said, 'I've got something to show you.' He led me into the garage, and there was a pile of human bones. He said the developers had unearthed an unmarked grave in their diggings, and he had rescued the remains and was going to have them reburied.

"Everything became clear to me all of a sudden. That was why Melanie had been calling for me to help. Her resting place had been disturbed. She had been trying to tell me that. I believe she might even have been worried that people would find out she was pregnant. I don't know for sure."

The young woman must have found peace at last with her reburial. And with it, Mary felt a tremendous relief. She never saw or heard the vision or the voice again.

The Sleeping Prophet

It would seem almost sacrilegious to write a book on haunted Virginia and not mention the extraordinary man from Virginia Beach who is widely recognized as the greatest psychic of the twentieth century—Edgar Cayce.

He was known as the "Sleeping Prophet," the "Psychic Diagnostician," and the "Miracle Worker of Virginia Beach." For more than forty years, Cayce helped save lives, cure ailments, and otherwise heal the sick through detailed readings he gave while in a trancelike state. Two-thirds of his more than fourteen thousand readings were medically related. Though he had no more than an eighth-grade education, Cayce, while asleep, somehow inexplicably had the amazing ability to envision and diagnose the ailments, no matter how complicated, of people all over the country.

Then, in precise, meticulous, and sophisticated detail, he would prescribe the medicines and treatments essential to regain full health. Often such prescriptions included lengthy and complex medical terminology, and at times obscure or long-forgotten remedies of which Cayce had no knowledge when awake. Astoundingly, of those cases verified by patients' reports, 85 percent of the diagnoses were found to be completely accurate, and those who followed the prescribed treatments got the results predicted in his readings.

To further his work for the benefit of mankind—Cayce never really profited in a material sense from his psychic powers—he founded, in 1931, the Association for Research and Enlightenment in Virginia Beach. Today the ARE, headed by his grandson Charles Thomas Cayce, has more than a hundred thousand members worldwide and is dedicated to physical, mental, and spiritual self-improvement programs through researching and applying the information in Edgar Cayce's psychic readings.

When he died in 1945, Cayce left behind a legacy of readings that have withstood the test of decades of intensive research and study. He remains the most documented psychic of all time.

Did he ever have any experiences with ghosts? The answer, says Charles Thomas, is yes. "I was only three when my grandfather died, so I can only tell you what I have heard from members of the family and friends. My late father, Hugh Lynn Cayce, and my uncle, Edgar Evans Cayce, mentioned stories about my grandfather communicating with spirits."

It has been written and attested to that when Cayce was a small boy, he saw and played with a whole gang of ghostly playmates. It was disappointing to him that adults could not see the "play people" with whom he had so much fun. His mother believed him when he told her about the invisible boys and girls. She was the one person in the world who completely understood him. It was reported, too, that the young Cayce seemed amazed that his spectral friends could run in the rain without getting wet, and he wondered why they always disappeared whenever grown-ups came near.

Cayce talked of seeing his own grandfather—after the man had died in a drowning accident. He said he sometimes saw manifestations of his grandfather in the barn. "Of course, Grandpa wasn't really there. You could see through him if you looked real hard."

He apparently had a number of encounters with ghosts during his adult years as well. Hugh Lynn Cayce remembered his father talking about such incidents. One night, there was a tapping on a downstairs window at their Virginia Beach home. "Edgar rose from his bed to go down and see what it was. It seemed to him perfectly natural to get up and go unlock the front door and let in a rather diffident young woman—who had been quite dead a few years!" The apparition told Cayce she had died but hadn't realized she was dead and was having a terrible time adjusting to the "other side." She had returned to see if he could help her. Hugh Lynn said, "He taught her how to release herself from what some people call the

'earthbound condition,' and to move forward in her path of devel-
opment. Edgar both saw and heard this woman. Actually, he saw
through her because she wasn't exactly solid."

Hugh Lynn, along with other members of the family, experienced spectral visitations once in their home. Shortly after Squire
Cayce, Edgar's father, died, they heard some "puttering around"
upstairs, mostly in a bedroom when no one was upstairs. "Edgar
told everyone not to worry, that it was just his father 'returning' to
straighten out some papers before he 'left' for good," says Hugh
Lynn. "Edgar said to just leave him alone and he would be gone
pretty soon."

But Hugh Lynn couldn't resist the temptation. "I just heard the
noise so clearly at lunch that I insisted on running upstairs to
check." As he reached the landing before getting to the top of the
stairs, he felt a presence that he described as "a cold area—a feeling
of cobwebs." He adds, "Every hair on my body stood at attention."

One evening in the fall of 1933, Cayce was alone downstairs in
his house, listening to the radio, when suddenly the room got icy
cold, and he felt something supernatural taking place. When he
looked toward the radio, he realized that a longtime friend of his—
a man who had been dead for several months—was sitting in front
of the radio. According to Cayce, "He turned and smiled at me, saying, 'There is the survival of personality. I know!' I was shaking all
over. He said nothing more and he just seemed to disappear. I
turned off the radio. It still appeared as if the room was full of some
presence. As I switched off the light and climbed the stairs, I could
hear many voices coming from the darkened room. Jumping in bed
and shivering from cold, I aroused my wife. She asked me why I
hadn't turned off the radio. I assured her that I had. She opened the
door and said, 'I hear it. I hear voices.' We both did."

The spirit of Edgar Cayce, who died in 1945, is said to have
appeared at least once. It happened in 1976. Gerry McDowell then
was a volunteer worker at ARE. She had finished a shift at her job,
and then decided to tackle some more paperwork in an adjacent
building. But she kept nodding off and was told to go outside in the
hallway and lie down on the couch—the same couch that Cayce
had used to sleep on for many of his readings.

"I guess I slept for about an hour," she recalls. "When I awoke,
there, standing over me, was a man. I had never seen Edgar Cayce

in life, but I recognized him immediately from his photographs. He was wearing a blue suit, a blue tie, and a white shirt. He smiled at me and I smiled back. He pointed a finger at me, and then he dematerialized. I went in and told the others in the office what had happened, and they said it meant he wanted me to stay; that I would never get away from here now."

Gerry McDowell didn't. She became a full-time staff member.

A Case of Crisis Apparition

It is a shaded isle of serenity amid the hustle and bustle of downtown Norfolk. It has been that way for more than 350 years. In fact, the first church built on the site of the present-day St. Paul's was known as "Ye Chappell of Ease." It was erected in 1643 as part of the Elizabeth River Parish. Norfolk became a borough in 1736, and the present church was built three years later.

It was struck and partially burned by the British on January 1, 1776, when Norfolk was bombarded and destroyed. The building was serving as a shelter for women and children during the attack. During the Civil War, the church was occupied by Federal forces from 1862 to 1865. In the yard are 274 listed graves, the oldest of which is that of Dorothy Farrell, who died on January 18, 1673. Some of the stone markers bear a skull and crossbones, which signified simple death, not the resting place of a pirate.

Wedged in the far northeast corner of the churchyard is an aboveground tombstone with a strange quotation carved into it. "Yes," says a church spokesman when asked, "that was a tragic case. The poor man lost his whole family. It is our only ghost story."

It also apparently was a classic case of "crisis apparition." This, say paranormal experts, occurs when one person, known as the "receiver," suddenly becomes aware that another person, the "transmitter," is undergoing a crisis. This may be in the form of pain, shock, emotion, or death, even though the transmitter may be some distance away, in some instances thousands of miles. The most common examples of such phenomena occur in times of war, when a mother, say, may report seeing or hearing her son at the moment he is wounded, often at the instant of his death. The theory is that the pain and shock trigger involuntary telepathic contact between son and mother, or transmitter and receiver.

David Duncan's crisis apparition occurred in 1823. Three years earlier, he had married Martha Shirley. Duncan was captain of the cargo schooner *Sea Witch*, and he took his bride on a honeymoon voyage to several Mediterranean ports. Afterward, they settled in Norfolk, and she gave birth to twins, Davis and Ann. Early in 1823, Duncan set sail on a merchant trip, carrying a cargo of lumber and animal hides.

On the night of May 12, the *Sea Witch* was anchored off the harbor of Genoa, Italy. Most of the crew had gone ashore to unwind, but master Duncan had stayed behind and was reading in his cabin from eighteenth-century poet Edward Young's book *Night Thoughts on Death and Immortality*. It was eerily apropos.

Thousands of miles away, a fire broke out in a bakery beneath the Duncans' residence. Martha desperately tried to escape with her children, but a rickety staircase collapsed, and they perished in the flames. At that precise moment, David Duncan was reading the poet's lines describing death as an "insatiate archer," when he envisioned a fire at the foot of the main mast. He raced from his cabin, and when he reached the deck, the fire seemed to flare up. In the midst of the illusory flames, he clearly saw the wraithlike form of his wife frantically clutching their son and daughter.

Her screams pierced the silence in the harbor. "David, David, save us!" she cried. And then, in a flash, she was gone, as was the fire. Although Duncan was crazed with anxiety, it was not until weeks later, when his ship finally docked at Norfolk, that he learned the awful horror of his illusion was real.

He placed a horizontal, raised tombstone, inscribed with Martha's name and the date of death, over the single gravesite in St. Paul's churchyard. On the stone, he also had the stonemaker carve the two lines of verse he had been reading when his three loved ones had died: "Insatiate archer, could not one suffice? Thy shaft flew thrice and thrice my peace was slain."

Bibliography

Books, Journals, and Newspapers

Biggs, Elizabeth. *Beyond the Limit of Our Sight*. Flint Hill, VA: Lelil Books,. 1978.

Harland, Marion. *Marion Harland's Autobiography*. New York: Harper & Brothers, 1907.

Harrison, M. Clifford. *Home to the Cockade City*. Richmond, VA: House of Dietz Publishers, 1942.

Holzer, Hans. *Ghosts*. New York: Black Dog & Leventhal Publishers, 2003.

Journal of American Folklore, 1907

Lee, Marguerite DuPont. *Virginia Ghosts*. Richmond, VA: William Byrd Press, 1930.

Loth, Calder, ed., *The Virginia Landmarks Register*, 4th ed. Charlottesville: University of Virginia Press, 1999.

Mullins, E. D. *Tales from South of the Mountain*. Johnson City, TN: Over Mountain Press, 1992.

Percy, Alfred. *The Devil in the Old Dominion*. Madison Heights, VA: Percy Press, 1965.

Richmond Enquirer, December 27, 1811.

Scott, James G., and Edward Wyatt IV. *Petersburg's Story—A History.* Petersburg, VA: Titmus Optical Company, 1960.

Stearn, Jess. *Edgar Cayce: The Sleeping Prophet*. New York: Doubleday and Company, 1967.

Sugrue, Thomas. *There Is A River*. New York: Holt, Rinehart, and Wilson, 1942.

Taylor, L. B., Jr., *The Ghosts of Virginia*. Vols. 1–12. Lynchburg, VA: Progress Printing.

Manuscripts

Works Progress Administration. Ferrum, VA: Blue Ridge Institute.

About the Author

L. B. TAYLOR JR. **IS THE AUTHOR OF MORE THAN THREE HUNDRED** national magazine articles and forty-five nonfiction books. A native of Lynchburg, Virginia, and a current resident of Williamsburg, he wrote about America's space programs for NASA and aerospace contractors for sixteen years. He became interested in paranormal phenomena as a result of his research for the book *Haunted Houses* in 1982 (Simon & Schuster) and has subsequently written twenty books on Virginia's ghosts.

Other Titles in the

Haunted Series

Other Titles in the
Haunted Series

Haunted Connecticut
by Cheri Revai • 978-0-8117-3296-3
Haunted Delaware
by Patricia A. Martinelli • 978-0-8117-3297-0
Haunted Illinois
by Troy Taylor • 978-0-8117-3499-8
Haunted Jersey Shore
by Charles A. Stansfield Jr. • 978-0-8117-3267-3
Haunted Maine
by Charles A. Stansfield Jr. • 978-0-8117-3373-1
Haunted Maryland
by Ed Okonowicz • 978-0-8117-3409-7
Haunted Massachusetts
by Cheri Revai • 978-0-8117-3221-5
Haunted New Jersey
by Patricia A. Martinelli and Charles A. Stansfield Jr.
978-0-8117-3156-0
Haunted New York
by Cheri Revai • 978-0-8117-3249-9
Haunted New York City
by Cheri Revai • 978-0-8117-3471-4
Haunted Ohio
by Charles A. Stansfield Jr. • 978-0-8117-3472-1
Haunted Pennsylvania
by Mark Nesbitt and Patty A. Wilson
978-0-8117-3298-7
Haunted Southern California
by Charles A. Stansfield Jr. • 978-0-8117-3539-1
Haunted Vermont
by Charles A. Stansfield Jr. • 978-0-8117-3399-1

WWW.STACKPOLEBOOKS.COM • 1-800-732-3669